THIS BOOK BELONGS TO

_____

TALKING

WITH

GOD

TALKING

WITH

GOD

A PRACTICAL PLAN
FOR PERSONAL PRAYER

DICK EASTMAN

Chosen

a division of Baker Publishing Group
Minneapolis, Minnesota

© 1978, 2002, 2021 by Dick Eastman

Published by Chosen Books
11400 Hampshire Avenue South
Bloomington, Minnesota 55438
www.chosenbooks.com

Chosen Books is a division of
Baker Publishing Group, Grand Rapids, Michigan

Printed in China

ISBN 978-0-8007-6213-1

Adapted from portions of *The Hour That Changes the World: A Practical Plan for Personal Prayer* by Dick Eastman

Unless otherwise indicated, Scripture quotations are from the New King James Version®. Copyright © 1982 by Thomas Nelson. Used by permission. All rights reserved.

Scripture quotations identified ESV are from The Holy Bible, English Standard Version® (ESV®), copyright © 2001 by Crossway, a publishing ministry of Good News Publishers. Used by permission. All rights reserved. ESV Text Edition: 2016

Scripture quotations identified KJV are from the King James Version of the Bible.

Scripture quotations identified NASB are from the New American Standard Bible® (NASB), copyright © 1960, 1962, 1963, 1968, 1971, 1972, 1973, 1975, 1977, 1995 by The Lockman Foundation. Used by permission. www.Lockman.org

Scripture quotations identified NLT are taken from the Holy Bible, New Living Translation, copyright © 1996, 2004, 2015 by Tyndale House Foundation. Used by permission of Tyndale House Publishers, Inc., Carol Stream, Illinois 60188. All rights reserved.

Cover design by Studio Gearbox

21   22   23   24   25   26   27   7   6   5   4   3   2   1

Contents

Introduction

In my early thirties I discovered the delight of spending time with God in prayer. Moved by Christ's appeal to Peter in Matthew 26:40, "Could you not watch with Me one hour?" I embarked on a journey of blessing that has touched every day since.

The challenge to set aside an hour a day to be with the Lord, in His Word, was born. Because of a special burden for world evangelization, my hour included a plan to pray for the nations each day, thus becoming a daily hour that let me partner with God in changing our world.

It is with my deep gratitude to the Lord for His blessing that this special adaptation of *The Hour That Changes the World* is being published. I believe God is raising up an entirely new generation of faithful, fervent warriors of worship and intercession who will truly change our world through their prayers. If they are like me when I started out, they will appreciate a few guidelines to help them begin and to stay faithful. I pray these pages will help.

In addition to the hundreds of thousands who have read the original book, the circle of prayer with twelve prayer focuses has been reprinted in magazines, newsletters, prayer guides and church bulletins. It has also been photocopied all over the world, often presented to groups with accompanying teaching, even in such places as Saudi Arabia, Iran, Syria, Jordan and Cuba. This training has touched people of various languages, including Chinese, Russian, Arabic, Swahili, Lingala, Farsi, Hindi, Indonesian, Tagalog, Nepalese, Burmese, Thai, Korean and Vietnamese, as well as more familiar languages like German, French, Spanish, Portuguese and Italian (to name only several).

In churches, communities and houses of prayer around the world, believers are also committing time each week in prayer to fill all 168 hours with nonstop praying. Truly something great from God must be at hand! The Church is certainly praying as never before.

Prayer is a marvelous mystery hidden behind the cloud of God's omnipotence. Nothing is beyond the reach of prayer because God Himself is the focus of prayer.

Prayer is the simplest act a creature of God can perform. It is divine communion with our heavenly Father. Prayer does not require advanced education. Knowledge is not a prerequisite to engage in it. Only an act of the will is required to pray.

But prayer is more. Prayer is the vision of the believer. It gives eyes to our faith. In prayer we see beyond ourselves and focus spiritual eyes on God's infinite power.

Prayer is also humankind's ultimate indication of trust in our heavenly Father. Only in prayer do we surrender our problems completely to God and ask for divine intervention.

Prayer is not optional. On the contrary, it is quite obligatory. Where there is an absence of prayer, there will be an absence of power. Where there is frequency of prayer, there will be a continuing display of God's power. God said, "If My people who are called by My name will humble themselves, and pray and seek My face, and turn from their wicked ways, then I will hear from heaven, and will forgive their sin and heal their land" (2 Chronicles 7:14).

How to Use This Book

Whether you are able to pray a full hour or only a few minutes, the purpose of this book is to give you a plan for prayer. Here are some ideas for how you can use the twelve prayer focuses on the following pages:

- Read each chapter to learn more about the twelve prayer focuses, their biblical context and ways to incorporate them during prayer.

- Invest one to five minutes (or more) on each prayer focus depending on how much time you want to schedule for prayer. Each chapter concludes with practical action steps, a prayer starter and additional Scripture for meditation and prayer.

- Instead of trying to go through all of the prayer focuses in one setting, go deeper with only a few.

- Prioritize a different prayer focus each day for twelve days.

- Search the internet for "the hour that changes the world prayer circle." There is also a copy of it in this book. Print a photocopy of the image to put in your Bible or notebook, or download the image to your mobile device for easy access wherever you are.

I cannot imagine a day without the worship and wonder of waiting on God's presence. I invite you to share in this joy. It could change your life, and your world as well. I'm convinced it will make your day!

Dick Eastman, international president,
Every Home for Christ

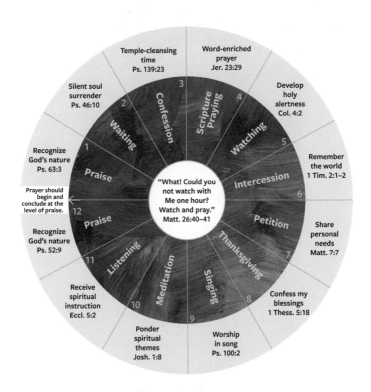

Recognize
God's nature
Ps. 63:3

Prayer should
begin and
conclude at the
level of praise.

Praise

1
2
3
4
5
6
7
8
9
10
11
12

"What! Could you
not watch with
Me one hour?
Watch and pray."
Matt. 26:40–41

1

PRAISE

THE ACT OF DIVINE ADORATION

Jesus left His disciples but a single prayer as an example upon which to base their praying. Although several of Christ's prayers are recorded in Scripture, only once did He say, "In this manner, therefore, pray." The prayer is recorded in its entirety in Matthew 6:9–13 and appears somewhat abbreviated in Luke 11:2–4. It is commonly called the Lord's Prayer, although the Disciples' Prayer would be a more accurate label. The first eight words of this important prayer provide the believer with a biblical foundation for commencing all prayer with a season of praise. The prayer begins, "Our Father in heaven, hallowed be Your name" (Matthew 6:9).

The goal of all praying is summed up in the expression "Hallowed be Your name." *Hallowed* is a New Testament expression used only in reference to the name of God. The Greek word for *hallow* is *hagiazo*, meaning "to revere or to sanctify." Since *sanctify* means "to set apart," our prayer time should include several moments, at the very outset, when God's name is set apart strictly as the object of our divine worship. During these moments of praise, our sole purpose is to bring glory to God with our words. God declared through the psalmist, "Whoever offers praise glorifies Me" (Psalm 50:23).

Praise is more than a single aspect of prayer. Praise is a way of life. The Westminster Catechism explains, "The chief end of man is to glorify God and to enjoy Him forever." Praise helps the believer achieve this "chief end." In fact, praise might well be the "chief end."

What is praise? Praise is the vocal adoration of God. Adoration is the act of rendering divine honor, esteem and love. The word *adoration* is derived from an ancient expression that meant "to apply the hand to the mouth," or "to kiss the hand." In certain countries a kiss of the hand is still a symbol of deep respect and submission.

The act of vocal adoration is important because it implies we acknowledge God as God.

Why Praise First?

Aside from the fact that Jesus listed praise first in His prayer, there are numerous reasons for placing it first when we pray. Only praise puts God in His rightful position at the very outset of our praying. In praising God we declare His sovereignty and recognize His nature and power.

Some have taught that confession should be first in prayer because sin makes effective praying impossible. True, sin does rob prayer of power. And confession is important. But were it not for a loving, merciful God, confession of sins would mean very little, regardless of when it was included during prayer. So, we must first draw our attention to God in prayer before we draw our attention to self.

Another major reason for offering praise early in prayer is the fact that, in its very nature, praise is unselfish. Making the decision to worship and praise God moves our attention from self to God. We soon discover spiritual health has its roots in divine adoration. Thus, praise is quite practical. It is practical because it changes our focus. As believers recognize God for all He is, they soon realize it is this all-powerful God to whom they will be presenting all of their later petitions.

Offering praise at the outset of prayer is also wise because of the biblical precedent given to praise. Praise sparks victory. Note the scriptural account of God's glory flooding His earthly temple: "When the trumpeters and the singers were to make themselves heard with one voice to praise and to glorify the LORD, . . . then the house, the house of the LORD, was filled with a cloud, so that the priests could not stand to minister because of the cloud, for the glory of the LORD filled the house of God" (2 Chronicles 5:13–14 NASB).

Not only does praise open our devotional hour to an outpouring of God's glory, but it promptly sends Satan running. He cannot tolerate the presence of God.

Where do we find God's presence? In Psalm 22:3 we are reminded that God inhabits "the praises" of His people. God manifests His living presence in the praise-saturated chamber of prayer. Adoration is the antidote to the poison of satanic oppression. To develop the "praise life" is to develop a certain immunity to the enemy's attacks. Satan is paralyzed in the presence of victorious praise.

Making the decision
to worship and praise God
moves our attention
from self to God.
We soon discover
spiritual health
has its roots
in divine adoration.

To Prize God

"Praise the Lord" is an expression commonplace in the vocabulary of most believers. But what exactly do we mean when we say, "Praise the Lord"? Basically, praise is the act of expressing one's esteem of a person for his or her virtues or accomplishments. It is to pronounce that person "worthy of honor."

But rendering praise to God is even more. The full meaning of praise can be captured only in its Old French origin, *preiser*, which means "to prize." To *praise* God is to *prize* God. The word *prize* means "to value, esteem, and cherish something." During our times of praise, we cherish and esteem God with our words of adoration.

Prize also means "to estimate the worth of." In praise, we mentally gather together all the facts we know about God and put these facts into words. Praise literally becomes "the fruit of our lips" unto God (Hebrews 13:15).

Because praise is to verbalize our esteem for God, it seems unlikely we will exhaust any potential list of possibilities for praise. The following are but a few scriptural suggestions for your moments of ministering unto the Lord through praise.

First, we should *praise God for His name*. The psalm-ist said, "Not unto us, O Lord, not unto us, but to Your name give glory" (Psalm 115:1). Although various titles describing God are shared throughout the Old Testament, the actual "name of the Lord" is not specifically revealed until the pages of the New Testament. His "name" is *the Lord Jesus Christ*. It greatly honors God when we take time during prayer to "prize" the name of Jesus Christ with words of praise. The Father loves the Son and wants us to love the Son, too.

When praising the name of Jesus in prayer, we may use expressions from Scripture, such as those used by Isaiah: "And His name will be called Wonderful, Coun-selor, Mighty God, Everlasting Father, Prince of Peace" (Isaiah 9:6).

Secondly, we should *praise God for His righteousness*. All that God is, deserves our praise. The psalmist intoned, "And my tongue shall speak of Your righteousness and of Your praise all the day long" (Psalm 35:28).

Righteous means "meeting the standards of what is right and just." God does more than meet certain standards—God *is* the standard. All that a prayer warrior can imagine concerning God's faithfulness, justice and mercy may become a theme for these moments of praise.

The possibilities
for praise
stretch beyond the limits
of our imagination.
Because God has no limit,
our praise is limitless.

Thirdly, we should *praise God for His infinite creation.* The psalmist said succinctly, "Praise Him for His mighty acts" (Psalm 150:2).

Because we are challenged to praise God for His "mighty acts," there is no limit to praise. God created countless species of plant and animal life, each serving as an individual basis for praise. The scope of praise ranges from the microscopic particles of the atom to the spiraling galaxies of the universe. All of creation is a treasure house of praise.

Finally, we should *praise God for His Word.* During moments of deep depression, King David wrote, "In God will I praise his word" (Psalm 56:10 kjv). Psalm 19 tells us some of the benefits of the Word of God:

1. "The law of the LORD is perfect, converting the soul."
2. "The testimony of the LORD is sure, making wise the simple."
3. "The statutes of the LORD are right, rejoicing the heart."
4. "The commandment of the LORD is pure, enlightening the eyes."

5. "The fear of the LORD is clean, enduring forever."

6. "The judgments of the LORD are true and righteous altogether."

Truly, the possibilities for praise stretch beyond the limits of our imagination. Because God has no limit, our praise is limitless.

Early in prayer take time to recognize all that God is. Express these thoughts vocally. And don't be in a hurry to go beyond praise until you have taken adequate time to adore God with your words of worship.

Lord, teach me to adore You!

Praise: The First Step in World-Changing Prayer

1. Always remember to start with praise.

2. Select a specific characteristic of God, such as His kindness, His patience or His righteousness.

3. Say out loud what comes to mind about that characteristic.

4. Expand your theme as much as possible. Allow God to reveal new themes for worship as your time of praise develops.

 **PRAYER**

Almighty God, I praise You for who You are—the omnipotent Creator who still takes time to know and love me. You are my Provider and my attentive Father. Today I want to specifically praise You for being [faithful, loving, my Healer, powerful . . .] and ask You to make me aware of how You manifest Yourself in this way around me.

SCRIPTURES TO PRAY

Psalm 103:1–5; Psalm 139:13–18; Philippians 4:8; Revelation 15:3–4

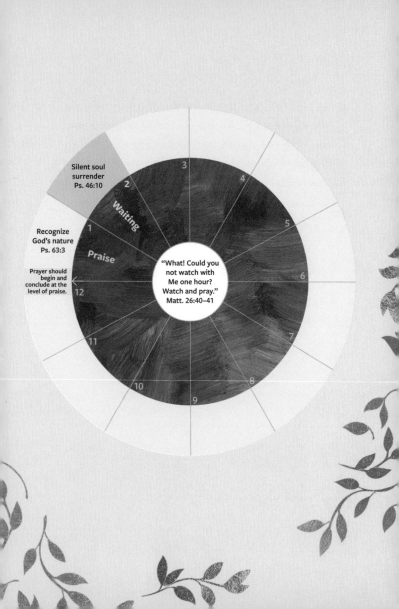

Silent soul
surrender
Ps. 46:10

Recognize
God's nature
Ps. 63:3

Prayer should
begin and
conclude at the
level of praise.

Waiting

Praise

3

4

5

6

7

8

9

10

11

12

1

2

"What! Could you
not watch with
Me one hour?
Watch and pray."
Matt. 26:40–41

2

WAITING

THE ACT OF SOUL SURRENDER

Few saints have longed after God with such sincerity as did Madame Guyon. Early in life, seeking spiritual encouragement, she approached a devout Franciscan friar. The young woman explained her desire for God had grown shamefully weak.

After hearing her story, the friar engaged in silent contemplation for a considerable time. Slowly the old Franciscan gazed up at Madame Guyon and declared, "Your efforts have been unsuccessful, because you have sought without only what you can find within. Accustom yourself to seek God in your heart, and you will not fail to find Him."[1]

Madame Guyon had received her introduction to a most vital element of prayer, that of silently waiting in the presence of God. All who would be used of God must learn this secret of silence.

A Dose of Silence

To be complete, prayer needs an early, significant dose of spiritual silence. Such silence is necessary if the believer hopes to minister effectively for Jesus. Just as virtue went out of our Lord when He ministered, a certain amount of spiritual virtue seems to depart believers during their daily ministry (see Luke 8:46). Recognizing this, we must seek renewal by communing with God.

What does it mean to wait upon God? And how does waiting differ from praise? Scripture includes numerous insights into the ministry of waiting: "I will wait on Your name" (Psalm 52:9). "My soul silently waits for God" (Psalm 62:1). "My soul waits for the Lord more than those who watch for the morning" (Psalm 130:6). "Those who wait on the LORD shall renew their strength" (Isaiah 40:31).

Waiting on the Lord is basically the silent surrendering of the soul to God. Waiting requires our total attention, focusing on hearing the voice of God.

Waiting is not praise, though it is closely related to praise and flows directly from it. Praise is verbalizing our esteem of God. Waiting is a time of silent love. Praise cries boldly, "God, I see these excellent qualities in Your nature." Waiting says softly, "God, I love You."

To a great degree our time of waiting might be termed "wordless worship." Being alone with God is the central issue of waiting. Genuine prayer is not merely asking for things; it is a relationship. Asking is only a part of prayer, and asking must come later. Strong relationships are best cultivated in silence.

It is also important to understand that our time of waiting is not necessarily a time of listening. Listening is crucial to prayer, but as with the aspect of asking, listening will come later. For now we simply surrender our hearts to the Lord in quiet love. In these silent moments we respond as Job: "What shall I answer You? I lay my hand over my mouth" (Job 40:4).

The Focus and Value of Waiting

John of Damascus, the ancient Greek theologian, defined waiting as "the elevation of the mind to God."[2]

Here we find the true focus of waiting. All attention must center on our heavenly Father. We come to know the Lord only at this most intimate level. The knowledge of God is best revealed in silent waiting. Scripture declares, "Be still, and know that I am God" (Psalm 46:10).

There is no power for prayer apart from God. Scripture does not say, "Have faith in prayer," but, "Have faith in God" (Mark 11:22).

Waiting on God is especially essential to prayer because it strengthens our knowledge and concept of God. To focus attention entirely upon God places God on the throne of our praying. Remember, we were not only challenged by the psalmist to "Be still," but to "know God" as well. Knowing someone intimately is impossible with limited attention. Intimacy takes time and concentration. This is why these early moments of prayer need a careful silencing of the mind, with all thoughts directed toward God alone.

Tragically, many believers become deceived by a spirit of selfishness that often follows them directly into the closet of prayer. Waiting helps deal with this spirit. It is an important step that prepares us for our time of confession, which is next on our list of prayer elements. Not only does waiting prepare the prayer warrior for confession, but it actually serves to snatch us away from the things of the world.

To wait in silence is to bid farewell to earthly conversation and attention. It is that vital bridge that takes us from a carnal world to a spiritual world. This silent surrendering of the soul to God opens the door to the "higher plane" of His divine love. Like any worthy spiritual vocation, waiting in prayer takes time. We must not rush these moments of spiritual silence.

We must wait for the best of God's blessings, even in prayer. Consider the case of Paul. When he surrendered his life to Christ, he immediately sought a mission: "Lord, what do You want me to do?" (Acts 9:6). And what was God's answer? He immediately sent Paul into the solitude of a quiet Arabian desert.

Building a friendship takes much time. The Bible says, "So the LORD spoke to Moses *face to face*, as a man speaks to his friend" (Exodus 33:11, emphasis added).

Little wonder Moses came from the mountain with his face shining. He met God "face to face." Here was a man who waited decades in a barren wilderness before catching a glimpse of the true glory of God. But, oh, the results of his lonely desert sojourn. Moses touched God, and God, in turn, touched Moses in those years of waiting.

Take Time to Wait

Concerning the importance of spiritual waiting, Andrew Murray wrote, "Here is the secret of a life of prayer. Take time in the inner chamber to bow down and worship; and wait on Him until He unveils Himself, and takes possession of you, and goes out with you to show how a man can live and walk in abiding fellowship with an unseen Lord."[3]

Especially strive to conquer the spirit of misspent conversation that permeates the very fiber of human life. Practice the art of silence throughout your day. Scripture declares, "Be silent, all flesh, before the LORD, for He is aroused from His holy habitation!" (Zechariah 2:13). Devote the early moments of your devotional hour to a time of silent sharing with the Lord. Wait patiently for a greater glimpse of His infinite glory.

Lord, teach me to wait!

Waiting: The Second Step in World-Changing Prayer

1. Bring your mind and spirit into a time of complete silence to the world.

2. Focus your thoughts on God the Father, His Son, Jesus, or the Holy Spirit.

3. If words are to be voiced, let them be quiet whisperings such as, "I love You, Lord," or, "I long for Your presence, O God."

4. Concentrate your full attention on the "love" aspect of God's nature in these minutes of silence.

 PRAYER

As I sit in silence before You, I am focused on Your love. Reveal Your heart to me while I wait for you.

 SCRIPTURES TO PRAY

Psalm 25:5; Psalm 27:14; Psalm 123:2; Isaiah 30:18

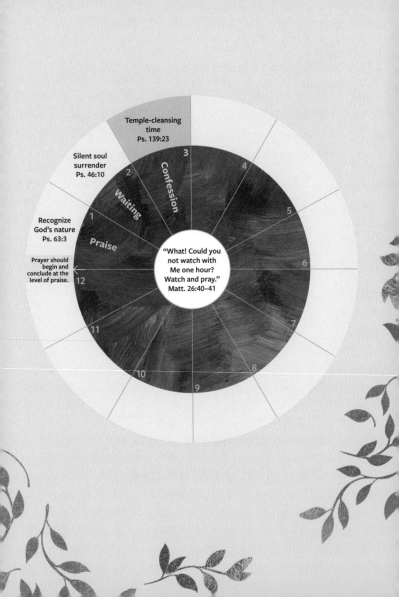

Temple-cleansing
time
Ps. 139:23

Silent soul
surrender
Ps. 46:10

Recognize
God's nature
Ps. 63:3

Prayer should
begin and
conclude at the
level of praise.

Confession

Waiting

Praise

3

2

1

12

11

10

9

4

5

6

7

8

"What! Could you
not watch with
Me one hour?
Watch and pray."
Matt. 26:40–41

3

CONFESSION
THE ACT OF DECLARED ADMISSION

Having honored God with vocal praise and silent love, we find the door now opens for truly effective praying. Immediately we must deal fully with the matter of personal sin. Andrew Murray reminds us, "God cannot hear the prayers on our lips often because the desires of our heart after the world cry out to Him much more strongly and loudly than our desires for Him."[1]

An awareness of our past failures especially tends to buffet the mind as we pray. Suddenly we feel hopelessly unworthy of offering our petitions. The devil has gained a victory and soon we stop praying altogether.

To combat these spiritual attacks we must take at face value all the promises of God concerning confession. "If we confess our sins," declared the apostle John, "He [God] is faithful and just to forgive us our sins and to cleanse us from all unrighteousness" (1 John 1:9). If unrighteousness renders our praying ineffective, then confession is the solution to the problem of sin-guilt in prayer.

What is confession? The New Testament Greek word for *confess* means "to agree with God" concerning His opinion of a matter. It also means "to admit my guilt." When we confess our sins, we are agreeing with God concerning the sin in our lives, as revealed through His Word by the Holy Spirit. Confession is to verbalize our spiritual shortcomings and admit we have sinned. Simply stated, confession is the act of declared admission.

At no other time in prayer does the believer look so carefully at his or her own spiritual growth as during confession. Both King David and Solomon spoke of this as communing with their own hearts. Dwight L. Moody called it a "personal debate betwixt ourselves and our hearts." Defining this aspect of prayer, Moody added, "Commune—or hold a serious communication and clear intelligence and acquaintance—with your own hearts."[2]

Heartfelt Recognition and Spiritual Cleansing

Confession is a heartfelt recognition of what we are. It is important to God because it indicates that we take seriously our mistakes and failures. Of course, God does not ask us to confess our sins because He needs to know that we have sinned, but because He knows that *we need* to know we have sinned.

This brings to our attention an essential law of prayer: *My prayer life will never rise above my personal life in Jesus Christ.* If my personal life is more worldly than godly, my prayer life suffers. The psalmist put it succinctly, "If I regard iniquity in my heart, the LORD will not hear" (Psalm 66:18).

According to Scripture there can be no effective prayer life where sin maintains its grip in the life of the believer. This is why confession is critical to our praying and should be implemented early in prayer. It clears the conscience of faith-killing guilt and opens the heart to truly believe God will hear our petitions.

Why is confession so difficult for some? Perhaps because confession is really the most painful part of personal prayer. The moment we admit that a particular act displeases God, we recognize the responsibility to change it. Immediately an inner battle of the will begins to take place.

This act of declared admission gives God access into the heart of a believer, removing all hindrances to effective prayer. There can be no healing *within* until there is first confession *without*. Confession is conditional to cleansing. Until known sin is fully dealt with, we are not ready to pray. As Christians our ultimate goal in prayer must be to glorify God by changing the world. God desires to pour Himself through us into our world, thus bringing about this change.

Herein lies the problem. How can a holy God pour Himself through a believer whose life is clogged with the debris of this world? Sin causes indifference, and it is impossible for indifferent people to change the world. Daily we must pray as the psalmist, "Search me, O God, and know my heart; try me, and know my anxieties; and see if there is any wicked way in me, and lead me in the way everlasting" (Psalm 139:23–24).

A careful study of Scripture reveals how important confession truly is. Those most mightily used of God were also those most willing to confess their weaknesses. Only after Isaiah cried, "I am undone," did the Lord invite him to serve. When Job confessed his sins and prayed for his friends, God changed his circumstances and gave him more blessings than during his greatest days of prosperity.

Daniel is another example. His life was so godly that the evil princes could find no fault in him (see Daniel 6:4). But note Daniel's awareness of personal sin. He wrote, "Now while I was speaking, praying, and *confessing my sin* and the sin of my people Israel, and presenting my supplication before the Lord my God for the holy mountain of my God, . . . the man Gabriel . . . reached me about the time of the evening offering" (Daniel 9:20–21, emphasis added).

These godly servants of ancient days had learned an important secret of power. The Holy Spirit works best through a clean vessel, and confession begins the process of cleansing.

The Why and How of Confession

Confession is not optional to spiritual growth. Through Isaiah God told His people, "Your iniquities have separated between you and your God, and your sins have hid his face from you, that he will not hear" (Isaiah 59:2 KJV).

Confession is crucial
for all spiritual growth,
not merely for effective prayer.
Before we will ever
willingly turn from sin,
we must first admit
that what we are doing
is sin.

Confession is crucial for all spiritual growth, not merely for effective prayer. It is that necessary "first step" to repentance. Before we will ever willingly turn *from sin*, we must first admit that what we are doing *is sin*.

During your times of confession, especially be on guard for little things—those unseen sins that grow to cause such severe damage. Every major spiritual failure begins as a tiny seed of misconduct.

A pattern for daily confession is found in Psalm 51. David prayed, "Create in me a clean heart, O God, and renew a steadfast spirit within me. Do not cast me away from Your presence, and do not take Your Holy Spirit from me" (Psalm 51:10–11). Here David provides a practical fourfold pattern for daily confession.

First, David cries out for *divine holiness*. "Create in me a clean heart," he pleads. I cannot be cleansed or forgiven by my own actions. Forgiveness is a work only God can do. So during confession I amplify David's request, elaborating on areas that I believe need improvement in my life. I quietly ask God to show me what needs cleansing.

Often a quick mental trip through the previous twenty-four hours reveals the need for confession. Ask yourself, "Did I fail God in any areas of personal conduct?" "Was I honest in my dealings with others?" "Were my thoughts pleasant to God?" As God reveals various spiritual short-comings, confess them and claim total victory.

Next, David cries out for a *divine attitude*. He continues, "And renew a steadfast spirit within me." Whereas David's first petition concerns a right relationship with God (a clean heart), this petition concerns a right relationship with others (a renewed spirit). One's attitude is crucial to dynamic praying. Bitterness toward others drains prayer of power.

A third quality ought to be sought during this aspect of prayer. David confessed his need for *divine guidance*. The king entreated, "Do not cast me away from Your presence." Here we confess our need for God's presence throughout the day, especially to defeat temptation. In the prayer Jesus gave His disciples, He taught us to pray, "Do not lead us into temptation" (Matthew 6:13). To confess my confidence that God will be with me when temptation comes helps prepare me for these attacks.

Finally, David cries out for *divine anointing*. Almost desperately the king confesses his need for the Holy Spirit: "Do not take Your Holy Spirit from me."

God certainly has no intention of removing His Spirit from obedient believers, but this aspect of confession is still important. It is a renewed affirmation that we cannot accomplish anything apart from the direct spiritual aid of the Holy Spirit. It is to admit that without God's Spirit operating in and through us, all efforts will be hopelessly ineffective.

Cleansing Your Spiritual Temple

To a great degree, confession in prayer is a time of spiritual cleansing. In ancient Bible days it was often necessary to clean and restore God's temple. Concerning the revival and restoration of the temple under Hezekiah, the Bible tells us, "Then the priests went into the inner part of the house of the LORD to cleanse it, and brought out all the debris that they found in the temple of the LORD to the court of the house of the LORD" (2 Chronicles 29:16).

Today, the dwelling place of God is not a temple of brick and mortar but the inner souls of human beings. Scripture declares, "Do you not know that your body is the temple of the Holy Spirit . . . ?" (1 Corinthians 6:19).

Confession is necessary to private prayer because it initiates the process of cleansing our spiritual temple. Allow enough time during prayer for a thorough cleansing.

Remember, confession in prayer is that final step that leads to confident praying.

Lord, teach me to confess!

Confession: The Third Step in World-Changing Prayer

1. Ask God to search your heart for any unconfessed sin.
2. Think about any recent activities that might be areas of spiritual failure that need confessing.
3. Confess any specific sins you may be guilty of, either against God or others.
4. Confess your need for divine guidance and supernatural strength to walk on God's narrow path of righteousness.

 PRAYER

All-knowing Father, I open up my life to Your inspection. Search my heart and reveal any areas where I am sinning against You or against others. Forgive

me and cleanse me of these sins. I humbly yield to Your divine guidance in every area of my life. Give me Your grace to walk in Your light and remain in Your presence.

SCRIPTURES TO PRAY

Psalm 32:5; Psalm 38:18; Psalm 51:1–17; Nehemiah 1:5–11

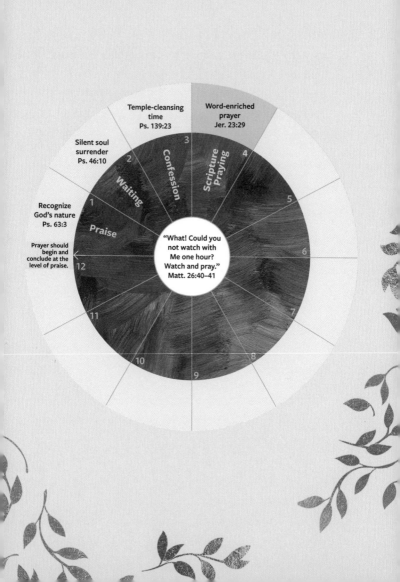

Temple-cleansing
time
Ps. 139:23

Word-enriched
prayer
Jer. 23:29

Silent soul
surrender
Ps. 46:10

Recognize
God's nature
Ps. 63:3

Prayer should
begin and
conclude at the
level of praise.

Confession

Scripture
Praying

Waiting

Praise

"What! Could you
not watch with
Me one hour?
Watch and pray."
Matt. 26:40–41

1
2
3
4
5
6
7
8
9
10
11
12

4

SCRIPTURE PRAYING
THE ACT OF FAITH APPROPRIATION

Although the Word of God is essential to the whole of our Christian experience, it is especially crucial to prayer. The degree to which we believe in God's Word and apply it to prayer is the degree to which God will pour out His power during our prayer.

We can never expect to grow in spiritual confidence if we spend little or no time getting to know God through His Word. Thus, God's Word must become an actual part of the devotional life. We may study the Bible throughout the week, but we should also seek to bring God's Word directly into our daily prayer.

Only as we systematically apply God's Word during prayer will we come to a full understanding of how much power God has made available to us.

"Prayer," said E. M. Bounds, "projects faith on God, and God on the world. Only God can move mountains, but faith and prayer move God."[1]

It is true that faith combined with prayer moves mountains, but where do we gain this mountain-moving faith? Paul reminded the Roman believers, "Faith comes by hearing, and hearing by the word of God" (Romans 10:17). In no other way is our faith strengthened as in familiarity with the Word of God.

Our prayer time, no matter how intense, is never truly complete without the divine nourishment available only from God's Word. Indeed, the Word of God is the Christian's true prayer book. It is our guide and foundation for all effective praying. To neglect God's Word is to neglect God's power.

Pleading God's Promises

Few leaders of the nineteenth century were known as much for their deep confidence in God and effectiveness in prayer as was George Mueller. At ninety years of age Mueller was able to declare, "I have never had an unanswered prayer." He claimed the secret to receiving answers to prayer lies in how the Christian applies God's Word during prayer. For example, George Mueller always prayed with an open Bible. He constantly filled his petitions with God's Word. Friends said the orphanage leader would not voice a petition without a "word from God" to back that petition.

In fact, Mueller never started petitioning God until *after* he nourished himself in God's Word.

Describing his devotional hour, George Mueller wrote, "The first thing I did, after having asked in a few words the Lord's blessing upon His precious Word, was to begin to meditate on the Word of God, searching as it were into every verse to get a blessing out of it; not for the sake of the public ministry of the Word, nor for the sake of preaching on what I meditated upon, but for the sake of obtaining food for my own soul. The result I have found to be almost invariably this, that after a very few minutes my soul has been led to confession, or to thanksgiving, or to intercession, or to supplication; so that, though I did not, as it were, give myself to prayer, but to meditation, yet it turned almost immediately more or less into prayer."[2]

George Mueller had learned the important secret of transforming God's Word into faith-filled petitions. He literally "prayed" the Word of God.

Charles Spurgeon was another noted leader who understood this secret. He expressed, "Every promise of Scripture is a writing of God, which may be pleaded before Him with this reasonable request, 'Do as Thou hast said!' The Creator will not cheat the creature who depends upon His truth; and far more, the Heavenly Father will not break His Word to His own child."[3]

The Word of God is more than a mere foundation for effective praying; it is the actual substance for effective praying. Just as the Word of God brings life to the believer's daily walk, God's Word brings life into our praying.

Concerning the power of Scripture, Paul declared, "For this reason we also thank God without ceasing, because when you received the word of God which you heard from us, you welcomed it not as the word of men, but as it is in truth, the word of God, which also *effectively works* in you who believe" (1 Thessalonians 2:13, emphasis added). The New Testament in Basic English declares that God's Word has "living power in you who have faith."

Years ago I discovered the amazing secret of prayer called "Scripture praying." In Paul's words to the Thessalonians

The degree to which
we believe in
God's Word
and apply it to prayer
is the degree to which
God will pour out
His power
during our prayer.

we find the basis for this mode of praying. If God's Word "effectively works" in those who believe, it should carry the same impact *within our prayers*. By bringing God's Word directly into our praying, we are bringing God's power directly into our praying.

The psalmist said, "I will never forget Your precepts, for *by them You have given me life*" (Psalm 119:93, emphasis added). Note God's promise given through Jeremiah: "'Is not My word like a fire?' says the LORD, 'And like a hammer that breaks the rock in pieces?'" (Jeremiah 23:29).

The Method of Scripture Praying

My experiences with Scripture praying began when I would listen to passages from Psalms and Proverbs during my hour of prayer. I quickly discovered that certain passages of Scripture prompted me to pray for specific needs. Before long I found that a definite plan for enriching my prayer with God's Word was developing.

Although I now simply use an open Bible in my daily devotional hour, systematically praying through Scripture a few chapters each day, you might find listening to Scripture helpful. Following is a simple three-step plan for Scripture praying that emerged in my daily program.

First, read (or listen to) a passage from God's Word. Try to include approximately *one chapter during each devotional hour.* Of course, you may focus on more than one chapter, but too lengthy a portion of Scripture may dilute the impact of Scripture praying.

Remember, in using this method of praying you are not actually studying the Bible for the sake of Bible study, but you are searching the Scripture for actual power that might be applied to your petitions.

Second, while reading Scripture, allow your finger to move slowly from verse to verse. The moment you discover a verse (or two) that impresses a particular truth upon your heart, *quietly meditate on what that verse is saying to you.* Ponder every aspect of this passage. This will usually happen in a matter of a few seconds. Carefully evaluate how the passage might be transformed into a specific petition. Ask yourself several questions. Does this verse prompt me to pray for something specific? How can this passage be directly applied to my petition? Is it possible to use some of the words of this Scripture, verbatim, as I pray?

Third, with these moments of meditation as a base, *form a personal prayer "enriched" by that promise from God.* In some cases you may read (or listen to) an entire

Our prayer time,
no matter how intense,
is never truly complete
without the divine nourishment
available only from
God's Word.

chapter before receiving a specific thought that will directly apply to a particular petition. But when that thought comes, use it to enhance your request. Mentally develop an actual prayer based on what you have read (or heard) in the passage and offer that prayer to the Lord.

As you develop this method of praying, keep in mind that it is not necessary to form a prayer for every verse of a chapter. In fact, some passages of Scripture are somewhat difficult to use in Scripture praying. For the most part, Psalms, Proverbs, the gospels or the Epistles provide the best setting for this method of praying.

Beyond Word-enriched prayer, the intercessor will find equal excitement in Word-enriched praise. J. Oswald Sanders, in his excellent book *Prayer Power Unlimited*, explains, "The Scriptures are rich in material to feed and stimulate worship and adoration—especially the Psalms, which are God's inspired prayer books. As you read them, turn them into prayer. Vast tracts of truth await our exploration. Great themes abound—God's holiness, sovereignty, truth, wisdom, faithfulness, patience, love, mercy—all of which will call forth our worship."[4]

As you begin to implement Scripture praying be careful not to neglect other important aspects of prayer. Remember, our goal as prayer warriors is to develop a devotional habit that is complete and well-balanced. Some may find the excitement of Word-enriched prayer so fulfilling that little time is given for other serious prayer matters. Be careful not to neglect intercession, listening, praise, thanksgiving and the other vital elements so essential to "complete" prayer. Yet, strive to give the Word of God its rightful place.

Lord, teach me to plead Your promises!

Scripture Praying: The Fourth Step in World-Changing Prayer

1. When bringing Scripture into your devotional hour, ask God to bless His Word to your spiritual body, just as He blesses natural food to your physical body.

2. Examine one of the Scriptures to Pray below, or another passage from the gospels, the Epistles, Psalms or Proverbs. Look for specific ways to apply each verse to prayer.

3. As you study a verse (or verses), ask yourself what petition this passage prompts you to make to God, or what promise this passage contains that stands directly behind a specific petition.

4. Develop actual prayers based on the thoughts and phrases included in a verse (or verses) of Scripture and offer those prayers confidently to the Lord.

 **PRAYER**

Thank You, God, for providing Your Word for my spiritual food. May it nourish me every time I take it in. As I read Psalm 91, I am reminded of the promise that You will take care of me. Protect me from evil and anything that would cause me harm. Give Your angels charge over me and deliver me. Thank You for the peace I can rest in knowing You are my refuge.

SCRIPTURES TO PRAY

Psalm 73:26; Psalm 91; Proverbs 3:24; Proverbs 4:5; Matthew 11:28; Mark 11:22–25; Luke 10:2; John 16:33; Philippians 1:9–11; Ephesians 1:17–19; Ephesians 3:16–19; Colossians 1:9–12

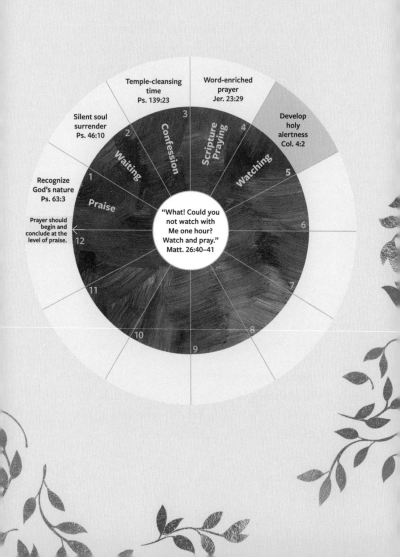

Temple-cleansing
time
Ps. 139:23

Word-enriched
prayer
Jer. 23:29

3

Silent soul
surrender
Ps. 46:10

2

Confession

Scripture
Praying

4

Develop
holy
alertness
Col. 4:2

Waiting

Watching

5

Recognize
God's nature
Ps. 63:3

1

Praise

"What! Could you
not watch with
Me one hour?
Watch and pray."
Matt. 26:40–41

6

Prayer should
begin and
conclude at the
level of praise.

12

7

11

8

10

9

5

WATCHING

THE ACT OF MENTAL AWARENESS

Books on prayer seldom discuss, or even mention, the importance of "watching" in prayer. Yet Jesus commanded us to "watch and pray!" (Matthew 26:41; Mark 14:38).

Paul also challenged believers to "Continue steadfastly in prayer, *being watchful in it* with thanksgiving" (Colossians 4:2 ESV, emphasis added). He made it clear that watching was to be a *specific element* of prayer, something as important to prayer as thanksgiving.

Be on the Alert

What did Jesus and His chief apostle mean when they challenged us to watch in prayer? The Greek word for our word *watch* is *gregoreo*, "to be awake or vigilant." The dictionary defines *watch* as "keeping awake in order to guard." It can also mean "a close observation" or "to be on the alert." When Jesus and Paul used the expression *watch*, they principally meant that believers should stay awake spiritually and keep guard. Since both Jesus and Paul linked watching with prayer, they were referring to staying alert during prayer, noticing the tactics of our enemy. When the apostle Peter warned us to be "vigilant" because Satan seeks to devour us (1 Peter 5:8), he used the very word *gregoreo* (translated "watch"), which both Jesus and Paul used in conjunction with prayer.

After Paul spoke to the Ephesian Christians about putting on the full armor of God, he again stressed watching. Paul suggested they establish everything by "praying always with all prayer and supplication in the Spirit, *being watchful to this end* with all perseverance and supplication for all the saints" (Ephesians 6:18, emphasis added).

During this activity of watching, our spiritual function is somewhat similar to the ministry of the watchmen in ancient Bible days. Concerning the city of Jerusalem, God said, "I have set watchmen on your walls, O Jerusalem; they shall never hold their peace day or night. You who make mention of the LORD, do not keep silent" (Isaiah 62:6).

Appointing watchmen to guard walled cities was a common custom in Bible days. The watchman's chief responsibility was to warn the inhabitants of approaching enemies. The thought in Isaiah 62:6 is that God's prophets were like these watchmen. They could not hold their peace until the prophecy of God was fulfilled in the full restoration of Jerusalem. These watchmen stood alert to warn of impending spiritual conflict.

Our first order of business during the watching phase of prayer is to make ourselves aware of the various ways Satan seeks to hinder the effectiveness of our prayer. From the earliest moments of prayer, he comes on the attack, trying to draw our minds from the key issues of prayer. To watch in prayer is to become aware of these attacks and stand firmly against them.

We should especially guard against prayer that lacks purpose. Suddenly the many items on our prayer list seem empty or vague. Prayer becomes shallow. We find ourselves making statements about prayer, instead of claiming specific things in prayer.

Only as we develop a spirit of watchfulness can we recognize Satan's plan of attack and block his efforts. But watching in prayer goes beyond developing an alertness to the manner in which Satan may attack. From a practical standpoint, time should be allocated during prayer for mental reflection concerning what is happening beyond our immediate world. Not only must we be alert to personal satanic attacks, but we must become aware of the "wiles of the devil" as they pertain to God's plan throughout the world.

Steps for Watching

Because watching means "a close observation," we must develop a plan for prayer that helps us observe the needs around us much more specifically. Following are several suggestions that should help intercessors develop just such a plan.

First, endeavor to read material that makes you spiritually aware of specific world needs. Missionary journals and denominational reports can be of great assistance in developing this awareness. Every Home for Christ, the ministry I direct, engages several staff members around the world who do nothing but research specific needs of world evangelism. Such research is of enormous value in helping to inform concerned intercessors. A good deal of "prayer fuel" is available to help Christians pray intelligently.[1] The tragedy is that so much of it is neglected due to a lack of awareness or outright unconcern.

Second, during prayer strive to reflect mentally about news of the day. Newspapers, as well as radio, television news broadcasts and the internet contain certain items that have a definite bearing on God's work throughout the world. Economic problems, civil unrest, political changes and even weather conditions can enter into the fulfillment of the Great Commission. Ask God to refresh your mind concerning current events that deserve special prayer attention.

Finally, and certainly most important, ask the Holy Spirit to show you exactly what you should claim in prayer and how you should claim it. None of the suggestions discussed in this book can be put fully to use apart from concentrated direction from the Holy Spirit. In fact, without the Holy Spirit guiding us, effectiveness in prayer is an impossibility.

Spiritual Prayer

No discussion of the subject of watching in prayer can be complete without emphasizing the value of the Holy Spirit

Because watching means
"a close observation,"
we must develop a plan for prayer
that helps us observe
the needs around us
much more specifically.

in prayer. Paul told Roman believers, "Likewise the Spirit also helps in our weaknesses. For we do not know what we should pray for as we ought, but the Spirit Himself makes intercession for us with groanings which cannot be uttered. Now He who searches the hearts knows what the mind of the Spirit is, because He makes intercession for the saints according to the will of God" (Romans 8:26–27).

It is clear from this passage that a prayer warrior is not left to himself in understanding the "how" of prayer. Each has been given the help of the Holy Spirit to guide and direct. This guidance is best cultivated in the watching aspect of prayer.

Twice in Scripture believers are admonished to "pray in the Spirit" (Ephesians 6:18; Jude 20). Of course, praying in the Spirit means vastly different things to different Christians. The purpose here is not to evaluate this expression from a theological standpoint. Numerous books have exhausted this subject quite well. However, I do suggest the reader seek to develop a much enlarged recognition of the Holy Spirit's power as it relates to personal prayer.

Praying in the Spirit leads to a deeper level of intimacy that awakens our minds and increases our understanding.

Perhaps the reason much of our praying becomes dull and lifeless is that we lack spiritual intimacy with the only Being who can add life to our praying.

God earnestly desires to reveal special secrets during prayer that help us pray more specifically for particular needs. To watch in prayer is to open our spiritual eyes to perceive these secrets. We must permit the Holy Spirit to enlighten us during prayer.

As we seek to watch in prayer, God will enlarge the capacity of our imagination to see certain needs even more clearly. Scripture says, "But as it is written: 'Eye has not seen, nor ear heard, nor have entered into the heart of man the things which God has prepared for those who love Him.' But God has revealed them to us through His Spirit" (1 Corinthians 2:9–10).

Paul is reminding us that spiritual insight does not emerge from the inner resource of our ability *unless* it is illuminated through the power of the Holy Spirit. This is why we must earnestly covet more of God's Spirit in our praying.

As we develop the ministry of watching in prayer, whether we set aside two minutes or ten, soon God will call upon us to pray very special prayers. We should expect to see things that startle us.

Professor Hallesby shared an account that illustrates this thought. He spoke of an ordinary country girl, Bolette Hinderli, who had a most unusual prayer experience that ultimately brought thousands to Christ.

While in prayer the young girl experienced an inner vision of a man in a prison cell. She observed his face as plainly as the print on this page. Accompanying this vision was an inner voice that urgently declared, "This man will share the same fate as other criminals if no one takes up the work of praying for him. Pray for him, and I will send him out to proclaim my praises among the heathen."

Bolette Hinderli was obedient to the heavenly call. For months she prayed earnestly that the prisoner would learn of God. She carefully searched news articles and listened to testimonies of converted Christians. She hoped to hear of someone converted while in prison and now proclaiming the Gospel.

Finally, during a trip to a distant city in Norway, Bolette Hinderli heard that a former prisoner, now converted to Christ, was scheduled to share the evening message in a local church. With quiet excitement Miss Hinderli sat in a pew, awaiting the message. Then, Lars Olsen Skrefsrud, the guest speaker for the evening, walked to the small pulpit. Bolette's heart exploded for joy. She immediately recognized the face of the man who preached. It was, without question, the very man for whom she had been praying.[2]

We must depend daily on the Holy Spirit to enlarge our awareness in all matters of prayer.

Lord, teach me to watch!

Watching: The Fifth Step in World-Changing Prayer

1. Take a few moments during prayer to become spiritually alert. Watch for the methods Satan may try to use to hinder your Christian walk today. Jesus has given you power to defeat Satan in each of these areas.

2. To become alert to specific needs around the world, go to EHC.org/resources to download helpful prayer resources. To access a prayer calendar for every nation, go to OperationWorld.org or download the Operation World app on your mobile device.

3. Prayerfully recall various international news developments that deserve special prayer.

Satan seeks to hinder
the effectiveness of prayer.
To watch in prayer
is to become aware
of these attacks and stand
firmly against them.

4. Ask the Holy Spirit to reveal further spiritual facts about these needs. This will aid you in praying more intelligently for these needs.

PRAYER

God of the Nations, today I am stopping to focus on You. I am sometimes distracted by unimportant things, worrying needlessly. Your Word tells me You will give me peace beyond understanding, and I claim that peace. I pray now for believers in the Middle East who are facing persecution. Send Your ministering angels to give them strength and courage. I also ask You to be with those in countries experiencing natural disasters, providing them protection and provision. Holy Spirit, You are welcome to speak to my heart and give me specific things to pray for in these situations. Thank You for being concerned about our needs and attentive to our prayers.

▬▬▬ **SCRIPTURES TO PRAY** ▬▬▬

Luke 8:24; Ephesians 6:10–13; Philippians 1:19;
Colossians 4:2–4

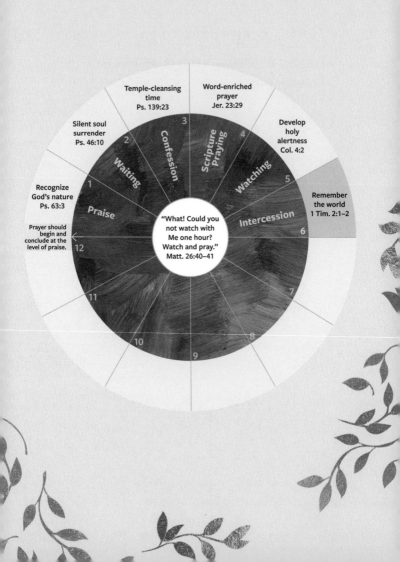

Temple-cleansing
time
Ps. 139:23

Word-enriched
prayer
Jer. 23:29

Silent soul
surrender
Ps. 46:10

Develop
holy
alertness
Col. 4:2

3

Confession

Scripture
Praying

4

2

Waiting

Watching

5

Recognize
God's nature
Ps. 63:3

1

Praise

Intercession

Remember
the world
1 Tim. 2:1–2

Prayer should
begin and
conclude at the
level of praise.

"What! Could you
not watch with
Me one hour?
Watch and pray."
Matt. 26:40–41

6

12

11

7

10

8

9

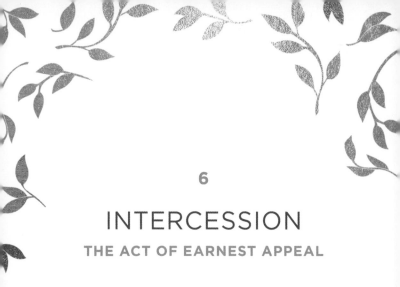

6

INTERCESSION

THE ACT OF EARNEST APPEAL

The follower of Christ knows his or her reason for being. We have both a divine purpose and a divine task. Our supreme purpose is to glorify God. Our supreme task is to evangelize the lost. In the truest sense, the latter most faithfully fulfills the former. To evangelize the lost glorifies God on the highest level.

This is why intercession (prayer for others) is so essential to the devotional habit. It might be labeled "the heart of prayer." Although intercession is only one facet of prayer, because of its importance, the concluding chapter will further develop this essential aspect of prayer.

No Higher Plane

What is intercession? It is God's method for involving His followers more completely in the totality of His plan. In no other way can the believer become as fully involved with God's work, especially the work of world evangelism, as in intercessory prayer.

Basically, intercession is prayer offered on behalf of another. When the prayer warrior intercedes, he or she forgets personal needs and focuses all faith and prayer-attention on others.

To intercede is to mediate. It is to stand between a lost being and an almighty God, praying that this person will come to know about God and His salvation.

Surely there is no higher plane for prayer than intercession. What could be more important than participating in the redemption of another being through prayer? True, our prayer does not save the sinner, but somehow it serves to prepare the heart for the moment word reaches the sinner of Christ's love. Search for a person who claims to have found Christ apart from someone else's prayer, and your search may go on forever.

The ministry of intercession, that of earnestly appealing on behalf of another, is especially important because it is the believers' common ground for Christian service. Spiritually speaking, prayer is the divine equalizer. Some preach, others teach, a few sing publicly, but all can pray.

Intercession is the broadest scope of prayer. There is no other mode of prayer that reaches out to all the world as does intercessory prayer. In intercessory prayer we find the key to freedom for those in bondage. Note the promise God gave Abimelech: "He [Abraham] is a prophet, and he will pray for you and you shall live" (Genesis 20:7).

Could it be that our very prayers hold "life" for the unevangelized? Those directly involved in world evangelism would answer a resounding yes. Ask almost any missionary if prayer is important in his or her labor and be prepared to hear a sermon.

Dr. Yohann Lee, onetime president of Every Home for Christ, is a Korean Christian who was born in China where his family once served as missionaries. During his tenure Dr. Lee saw more than eight million written decisions result from home-to-home literature evangelism.

To what did Lee attribute these extraordinary results? Speaking specifically on the steadfastness of these many converts, Lee said, "The prayers of the saints directly affect the proportion and degree of the Holy Spirit's power over a newborn babe in Christ. *Prayer is where it all begins and where it all ends.*"[1] Arthur T. Pierson adds, "Every step in the progress of missions is directly traceable to prayer. It has been the preparation for every new triumph and the secret of all success."[2]

But intercession is much more than merely praying for others. Interceding is engaging in actual battle.[3] There is a certain spirit of authority that must accompany a good deal of intercession. In that authority, we take back the ground the enemy has gained. This thought is amplified by A. J. Gordon, "We have authority to take from the enemy everything he is holding back. The chief way of taking is by prayer, and by whatever action prayer leads us to. The cry that should be ringing out today is the great cry, 'Take, in Jesus' great Name!'"[4]

Christ gave His life for those in the most remote places on earth. "The earth is the LORD's, and all its fullness" (Psalm 24:1). Satan has staged only a temporary invasion. Intercessors hold the power and authority to claim back what rightfully belongs to God.

True, God could save the world in a moment, but He waits for praying saints to join Him in the battle. This is *His plan,* and those who believe God answers prayer must be at the heart of it.

But to be at the heart of God's plan for world evangelization requires much more than mere lip service. As intercessors we must go beyond the simple act of praying for others, to the point of manifesting a genuine spirit of concern for others. Consider the example of Christ. Before our Lord ascended to heaven for the purpose of interceding on our behalf (see Romans 8:34), He first *gave Himself* to die on a lonely cross.

Thus, intercession begins with a spirit of giving before it becomes a spirit of praying.

Prayer Centered on Others

When Jesus taught His disciples to pray, it was clear the emphasis was to be on others (see Matthew 6:9–13). His prayer began with the plural possessive pronominal adjective—"our." We were not taught to pray, "*My* father," but, "*Our* Father!" Further in the prayer we see statements like "give *us*," "lead *us*" and "forgive *us*." In the deepest sense, the prayer is a love prayer. Every word is selfless. It cannot be prayed without deep compassion.

John Calvin declared, "Our prayer must not be self-centered. It must arise not only because we feel our own need as a burden which we must lay upon God, but also

There is no other
mode of prayer
that reaches out
to all the world
as does intercessory prayer.
In intercessory prayer
we find the key
to freedom
for those in bondage.

because we are so bound up in love for our fellow men that we feel their need as acutely as our own. To make intercession for men is the most powerful and practical way in which we can express our love for them."[5]

To keep our praying always centered on others, intercession should come before petition. Because Jesus realized we would periodically lapse into a spirit of selfishness, He taught us to pray, "Your kingdom come," before praying, "Give us this day our daily bread." Jesus wanted us to become "soul conscious" instead of "thing conscious."

When believers begin praying daily for unevangelized nations, it is not uncommon for their praying to sound strangely similar. After several weeks, or even just a few days, questions may arise concerning the matter of repetition in prayer. Is it wrong to repeat a prayer that is exactly the same as or similar to a prayer we have prayed previously? What did Jesus mean when He cautioned His followers concerning "vain repetition" in prayer?

Look carefully at the passage in question. Jesus said, "And when you pray, do not use vain repetitions as the heathen do. For they think that they will be heard for their many words" (Matthew 6:7).

Some Bible teachers use this verse to suggest that all repetition in prayer is unscriptural. But look again at our

Lord's exact words. Jesus did not actually condemn *all* repetition in prayer. Instead, He instructed His followers to avoid "vain" or "empty" repetition. He further qualifies the term *vain* by adding, "as the heathen do." These four words reveal what kind of repetition is meaningless in prayer.

Various heathen cultures have strange and unique forms of prayer that are clearly empty and repetitious. The Tibetan Buddhist prayer wheel is most notable. Chiseling prayers to heathen gods on a clay wheel, and assuming that spinning the wheel causes these hundreds of prayers to rise simultaneously during each revolution, is a perfect example of "vain" repetition.

On the other hand, Christians in right standing with Jesus, who bring before the Lord a similar petition from day to day, hardly find themselves in the same category as a wheel-spinning Buddhist. To pray similar prayers daily for various nations of the world cannot be classified as "vain" repetition. True, it may appear repetitious, but it is not vain.

The reader may be surprised to discover that repetition in prayer is even scriptural. In fact, Abraham failed in prayer because he gave up in his petitioning (see Genesis 18:16–33). However, Elijah pleaded with God seven times and witnessed a remarkable outpouring from God (see 1 Kings 18:42–45). Further, it is interesting to note that even our Lord repeated a prayer. In Gethsemane Christ offered a petition three times, "saying the same words" (Matthew 26:44). Twice Jesus prayed for a blind man (see Mark 8:24–25). King David repeated a "prayer of praise" twenty-six times in Psalm 136.

Making Mention in Prayer

After spending numerous times in prayer with a former associate in our ministry, I was amazed to find that he prayed for every person on the Every Home for Christ headquarters staff by name. He also prayed for each overseas leader associated with the ministry. Quietly and confidently he would appeal for compassion, wisdom and strength for each of the scores of workers on his list. Wives of these workers were also included.

Then, with continuing confidence, he prayed for every major Christian leader who was even vaguely familiar to me. And there was more. He proceeded to intercede for every king, president and political leader of the almost fifty Islamic and Communist nations at that time. He did not pray for the leaders collectively, but for each separately, *by name*.

Although the intensity and confidence of this praying blessed me, I realize some believers are troubled by the thought of lengthy prayer lists. They feel they are short-changing a need by simply "mentioning" the need briefly in prayer. Fortunately for my own prayer life, God directed my attention to a firm scriptural foundation for this very method of praying.

Not once, or twice, but four specific times the apostle Paul spoke of "making mention" of his fellow Christians in prayer. To Roman believers he wrote, "For God is my witness . . . that *without ceasing I make mention* of you always in my prayers" (Romans 1:9, emphasis added).[6]

Surely the apostle did not spend his entire waking time praying for every specific need of each fellow Christian. Instead, he confidently lifted their names before God, fully trusting God to bless each of them.

Never be troubled by the fact that your knowledge of a need is somewhat limited. True, you should ask the Holy Spirit to aid you in prayer so that your praying is as meaningful and intelligent as possible. But don't become discouraged solely because your prayers lack the depth of

Satan has staged
only a temporary invasion.
Intercessors hold
the power and authority
to claim back
what rightfully
belongs to God.

understanding you desire. Above all, remember that all of prayer, especially intercession, is a learning experience.

Lord, teach me to intercede!

Intercession: The Sixth Step in World-Changing Prayer

1. Prepare for intercession by developing a plan that includes prayer for God's work around the world. Go to EHC.org/resources to download helpful prayer resources. To access a prayer calendar for every nation, go to OperationWorld.org or download the Operation World app on your mobile device.

2. Ask God for a new compassion for these moments of intercession, so your praying will reach out to the lost with genuine concern.

3. Fill your intercession with the four key scriptural claims: Ask God to give more laborers to the harvest, to open doors for these workers, to bless them with fruit as the result of their efforts and to provide finances to expand their work. (See the concluding chapter for an explanation of these claims.)

4. Always try to include specific countries and their leaders during your time of intercession.

 **PRAYER**

Compassionate Father, I ask that You give me the heart of Christ so that I am aware of the needs around me and tender to the cries of humanity. Send laborers into the field to reach the lost, opening doors for them as they go. May the work of their hands be multiplied as You go before them and prepare the way. Provide for them financially and give them boldness to follow Your direction. Lord, I pray now specifically for the country of . . . , that You would hold the heart of their leader in Your hand and send revival to their land.

SCRIPTURES TO PRAY

Psalm 2:8; Matthew 9:38; Ephesians 6:18–20; 1 Timothy 2:1–2; Daniel 9:4–19

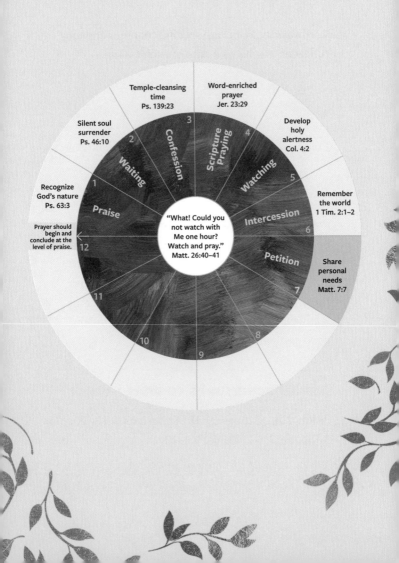

Temple-cleansing
time
Ps. 139:23

Word-enriched
prayer
Jer. 23:29

Silent soul
surrender
Ps. 46:10

Develop
holy
alertness
Col. 4:2

Recognize
God's nature
Ps. 63:3

3

Confession

Scripture Praying

4

Waiting

2

1

Watching

5

Praise

Intercession

6

Remember
the world
1 Tim. 2:1–2

Prayer should
begin and
conclude at the
level of praise.

12

"What! Could you
not watch with
Me one hour?
Watch and pray."
Matt. 26:40–41

Petition

Share
personal
needs
Matt. 7:7

11

7

10

8

9

PETITION

THE ACT OF PERSONAL SUPPLICATION

Petition is that aspect of prayer given over to asking God for specific personal things. To seek an unselfish spiritual or material blessing is not unscriptural. An Old Testament passage illustrates this. More than five hundred individual names are mentioned in the opening chapters of 1 Chronicles. Yet, amid this somewhat exhaustive genealogy, God pauses to provide a brief look at one of these individuals, a man named Jabez.

The Bible says, "Now Jabez was more honorable than his brothers, and his mother called his name Jabez, saying, 'Because I bore him in pain.' And Jabez called on the God of Israel saying, 'Oh, that You would bless me indeed, and enlarge my territory . . . and that You would keep me from evil, that I may not cause pain!' So God granted him what he requested" (1 Chronicles 4:9–10).

Nothing is mentioned about Jabez in Scripture other than that he sought a personal blessing of God and that it was granted. Such a testimony is not recorded of anyone else on this list of five hundred. Jabez was bold enough to entreat of God a blessing. God not only honored the request, but chose to use Jabez as an eternal example of how He longs to answer our sincere petitions.

The Rule of God

It is well said that "asking is the rule of the kingdom." The author of this statement, Charles Spurgeon, adds, "It is a rule that will never be altered in anybody's case. If the royal and divine Son of God cannot be exempted from the rule of asking that He may have, you and I cannot expect to have the rule relaxed in our favor. God will bless Elijah and send rain on Israel, but Elijah must pray for it. If the chosen nation is to prosper, Samuel must plead for it. If the Jews are to be delivered, Daniel must intercede. God will bless Paul, and the nations shall be converted through him, but Paul must pray. Pray he did without ceasing; his epistles show that he expected nothing except by asking for it."[1]

In the same sense that our Christian experience is a "personal" experience, prayer, too, must become very personal. We must not hesitate to declare as Jabez, "Bless me, indeed!" When Jesus faced the blind man, He asked, "What do you want Me to do for you?" (Mark 10:51). Certainly our Lord knew the man's infirmity, but He wanted him to declare it. This is petition. It is the confession of helplessness in a specific matter.

In a practical sense, petition is not the prayer of a person opening heaven's doors to release God's power. Rather, it is a person opening his or her heart's door to receive power already appropriated by God. Expressed helplessness is the key to opening that door, thus giving God access to our need. *We must define the need.* Because petition is an expression of helplessness, it should be present each day in the devotional hour. Jesus taught us to pray, "Give us *this day* our daily bread" (Matthew 6:11, emphasis added).

It is evident we are to express our dependence on Christ for every need. Personal petition is our means of such expression. During this aspect of prayer we are able to do as Job did when he "ordered" his cause before the Lord (Job 23:3–4 KJV). We go before God as an attorney with a carefully prepared argument upon which to base our case. We have a sincere, unselfish basis for our requests. Our motive is pure and our arguments well ordered. Of course, to bring our arguments before God in prayer does not mean we are twisting God's arm in order to obtain a particular blessing. God desires that we present these arguments because we will learn the principles of prayer only by the actual practice of prayer. This may also be the reason God sometimes delays an answer to our prayers. He longs to answer our petitions, but He also desires to teach us much more about matters of true spiritual warfare. This prepares us for the really serious battles that lie ahead.

Keys to Petition

When offering personal petitions, there are several principles that should be remembered.

First, *a petition should be specific*. Prayer must never be so vague that within minutes of our praying we have forgotten why we prayed. To forget our purpose for praying is a sure indication of an absence of desire. The greater the intensity of our desire for a blessing, the greater the difficulty to blot the desire from our mind. If we can't remember what we asked for after we asked for it, perhaps we really didn't need it.

Next, *a petition should be complete*. Each request ought to be carefully thought through before it is presented. Avoid shallow petitions like, "Lord, bless me," or, "Lord, help the missionaries today." Instead, pray carefully through each request. It is spiritually healthy to take a need apart, piece by piece, during prayer. Analyze the problem from every angle and then express it as a petition. The more specific and complete the petition, the more faith is generated when we bring it to God.

Third, *a petition should be sincere*. Personal attitudes are important in the matter of petition. It is true Jesus promises blessings to those who ask, seek and knock, but we must strive to bring our claims before God with a right spirit. How sincere are we when we seek a specific blessing of God? Insincere praying is selfish praying.

Finally, *a petition should be simple*. Although it was suggested earlier that we should analyze a problem, piece by piece, our manner of petition ought to be simple and informal. Long before an infant expresses its inner feelings in words, it cries out from within, expressing needs in the simplest of terms. The offering of a petition should be complete enough to build faith, but simple in its expression. Eloquence is not necessary for effective praying.

Even the simplest petition, when offered in faith, opens doors to the miraculous. God is greatly pleased when we come before His presence ready to ask of Him those petitions that will honor His name.

Lord, teach me to ask!

Petition: The Seventh Step in World-Changing Prayer

1. Begin your petitions by asking the Holy Spirit to help you claim only those desires that will bring honor to the Lord.

2. Make a mental list of specific needs you have for that very day and offer each need to God.

3. Focus on one petition, taking time to explain to God why you desire an answer for that request.

4. As you lean into your request by faith, occasionally examine your motives for claiming a petition. Be certain they are pure in the sight of God.

 **PRAYER**

Holy Spirit, purify my motives so that my heart's desire is to bring honor and glory to the Lord alone. I bring before You today my need. I ask that You would be merciful to me and bless me. May Your face smile with favor upon me. You are my Savior, Healer, Comforter and Friend. You provide for every need according to Your riches in Christ Jesus. I ask that the result of Your blessing my life is that people all over the world know You and serve You.

SCRIPTURES TO PRAY

Psalm 28:2; Psalm 67; Psalm 86:6; Philippians 4:6; 1 John 5:14–15

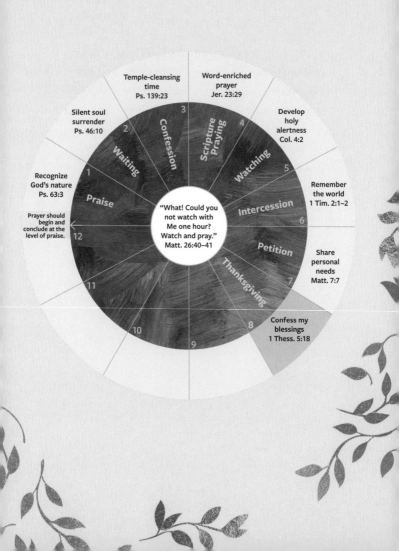

Temple-cleansing time
Ps. 139:23

Word-enriched prayer
Jer. 23:29

Silent soul surrender
Ps. 46:10

Develop holy alertness
Col. 4:2

3

Confession

4

Scripture Praying

2

Waiting

Watching

5

1

Recognize God's nature
Ps. 63:3

Praise

Intercession

Remember the world
1 Tim. 2:1–2

6

Prayer should begin and conclude at the level of praise.

12

"What! Could you not watch with Me one hour? Watch and pray."
Matt. 26:40–41

Petition

Share personal needs
Matt. 7:7

Thanksgiving

7

11

8

Confess my blessings
1 Thess. 5:18

10

9

8

THANKSGIVING

THE ACT OF EXPRESSED APPRECIATION

Although closely related to praise, thanksgiving itself is an important element that deserves careful attention during prayer. Basically, thanksgiving is the act of expressing specific gratitude to God for blessings He has bestowed upon us. These expressions may be mental or vocal.

Thanksgiving differs from praise in that praise focuses on *who God is*, whereas thanksgiving focuses on *what God has done* for us.

The Attitude of Thanksgiving

The precise position for thanksgiving on our prayer schedule may vary. A look at Scripture seems to suggest thanksgiving could be sprinkled throughout our praying. Paul told the Colossians, "As you therefore have received Christ Jesus the Lord, so walk in Him, rooted and built up in Him and established in the faith, as you have been taught, abounding in it with thanksgiving" (Colossians 2:6–7). Later, he added, "Devote yourselves to prayer, keeping alert in it with an attitude of thanksgiving" (Colossians 4:2 NASB).

Paul had a similar message for the church at Philippi. He instructed these believers: "Be anxious for nothing, but in everything by prayer and supplication, with thanksgiving, let your requests be made known to God" (Philippians 4:6). According to Paul, all prayers should be filled with a spirit of thanksgiving.

Thanksgiving might well be labeled "a confession of blessings." It is during this aspect of prayer that we recognize all of life's blessings and confess them before God. This is essential to prayer because it draws the heart to God, keeping it entirely centered on Him. Like praise, thanksgiving takes the believer's attention from self and places it where it must be centered to make prayer effective.

Thanksgiving is also important because it is the prayer warrior's special gift to God for His kindnesses. What else can we possibly give God other than praise and thanksgiving? The psalmist declared, "What shall I render to the LORD for all His benefits toward me?" (Psalm 116:12). Later, he answers, "I will offer to You the sacrifice of thanksgiving, and will call upon the name of the LORD" (Psalm 116:17).

In looking at the life of Christ, it is evident that a spirit of thanksgiving was important to Him. In the gospels we frequently see our Lord expressing gratitude. Describing the resurrection of Lazarus, the apostle John records, "Then they took away the stone from the place where the dead man was lying. And Jesus lifted up His eyes and said, Father, *I thank You* that You have heard Me" (John 11:41, emphasis added). Note Mark's description of Jesus feeding the multitude: "And He took the seven loaves *and gave thanks*" (Mark 8:6, emphasis added).

On yet another occasion, after sharing important teaching with His disciples, Jesus paused to pray, "*I thank You*, Father, Lord of heaven and earth, that You have hidden these things from the wise and prudent and have revealed them to babes" (Matthew 11:25, emphasis added). Surely that which was so important to our Savior should be considered essential to our devotional habit.

Offerings of Thanksgiving

A wandering mind normally hinders effective praying, but if properly channeled it actually can prove helpful during your time of thanksgiving. Allow your mind to wander through the previous day's activities. This will lead you to many points of concentration for specific thanksgiving.

Also, become aware of all that exists around you. What do you see worthy of thanksgiving? In the same sense that we need to watch in prayer or become alert to certain needs, we need to watch in thanksgiving. Become more aware of those specific things Jesus has done for you. Then verbalize these blessings. Remember, thanksgiving begins when you mentally catalog the specific things God has done for you so you can put these blessings into words.

Following is a brief list of several offerings of thanksgiving you might give God during your devotional hour:

First, *confess spiritual blessings*. What specific spiritual blessings has God given you recently? Perhaps He has bestowed a special blessing during this very devotional hour that is worthy of appreciation. Take time during prayer to offer these blessings back to God in the form of vocal thanksgiving.

Thanksgiving begins
when you mentally catalog
the specific things
God has done for you
so you can put these
blessings into words.

Second, *confess material blessings*. A moment should be given to consider the many material blessings God has generously provided. Be very specific, remembering even the little things. Thank Him for the chair in which you sit or the warmth of the room. The more specific thanksgiving becomes, the more meaningful a role it will play in your devotional life.

Third, *confess physical blessings*. We should thank God specifically for good health. If we are free of pain or sickness, it is a blessing worthy of thanksgiving. If we are experiencing pain in one leg, we can express appreciation for strength in the other. We may thank God for good eyesight or for the ability to hear. Each heartbeat or breath of air can be reason for thanksgiving. Like praise, thanksgiving is truly limitless.

Finally, *confess external blessings*. Some blessings are not directly related to us, but still they deserve an expression of appreciation. These might be termed external blessings. For example, thank God for kindnesses rendered to your friends, community or nation. Above all, thank Him for His blessings on the work of evangelism around the world. But especially strive to escape the tendency of generalized thanksgiving. Rather than declaring, "God, I thank You for blessing our church service last

Sunday," magnify your thanksgiving. Let it include specific reasons why you are thankful.

Thanks for Past Blessings

An especially meaningful goal of thanksgiving is to thank God each day for at least one blessing you cannot remember thanking Him for previously. This will require a moment of quiet contemplation concerning God's goodness.

In seeking a point of focus for this type of thanksgiving, you may wish to look at past experiences. Perhaps God granted you specific favor or some particular blessing decades ago for which you never expressed thanks.

Do you recall ever thanking God specifically for the person who first told you about Jesus? Have you thanked God for your first Bible, or for the Sunday school teachers who encouraged you in your early years of faith?

Thanksgiving is further described as limitless by Paul's admonition to the Ephesian believers, "Be filled with the Spirit . . . giving thanks always for all things to God" (Ephesians 5:18, 20). To the Thessalonians Paul adds, "In everything give thanks; for this is the will of God in Christ Jesus for you" (1 Thessalonians 5:18).

In each situation of life, no matter the difficulty it presents, focus for thanksgiving can be discovered. Even the death of a loved one reminds us of the knowledge of eternal life, something for which we are truly thankful.

Let us carefully seek to develop this ministry of expressing appreciation to God during prayer. For every specific prayer of petition, may we share two or three specific expressions of thanksgiving. God grant that we never cease to be grateful for His bountiful provisions.

Lord, teach me to give thanks!

Thanksgiving: The Eighth Step in World-Changing Prayer

1. Begin thanksgiving by thinking about all God has given you recently or in the past. You may want to create a written list.

2. Specifically thank Him for spiritual, material, physical and external blessings.

3. Frequently thank God in advance for blessings you expect Him to bestow on you in the future.

4. Thank God for at least one particular blessing you have not thanked Him for recently.

 **PRAYER**

God of endless blessings, I thank You for how You have provided for me recently. I see Your hand at work in my life in these specific ways. . . . I am appreciative of the prayers You are already answering, and for the peace I have in knowing You are taking care of my every need. Thank You for Your presence in my life and for role models who have helped me mature in my faith. I thank You for my health, my home, my family and friends, and my spiritual family. May I ever be mindful of the many blessings You pour into my life.

SCRIPTURES TO PRAY

1 Chronicles 16:34; Psalm 107:8–9; Psalm 116:17; 1 Thessalonians 5:18

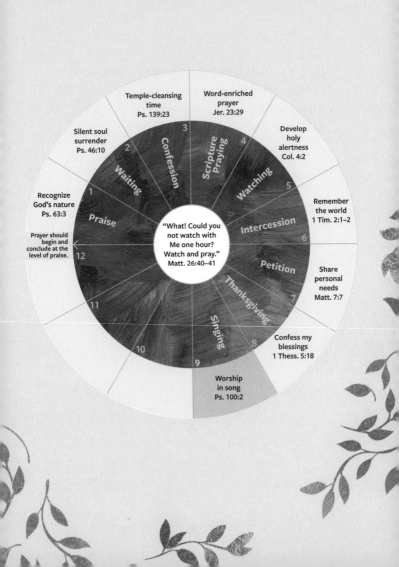

Temple-cleansing time
Ps. 139:23

Word-enriched prayer
Jer. 23:29

Silent soul surrender
Ps. 46:10

Develop holy alertness
Col. 4:2

Recognize God's nature
Ps. 63:3

Remember the world
1 Tim. 2:1–2

Prayer should begin and conclude at the level of praise.

Share personal needs
Matt. 7:7

Confess my blessings
1 Thess. 5:18

Worship in song
Ps. 100:2

3 Confession

4 Scripture Praying

2 Waiting

Watching

1 Praise

5

Intercession

6

"What! Could you not watch with Me one hour? Watch and pray."
Matt. 26:40–41

12

Petition

7

11

Thanksgiving

10

Singing

8

9

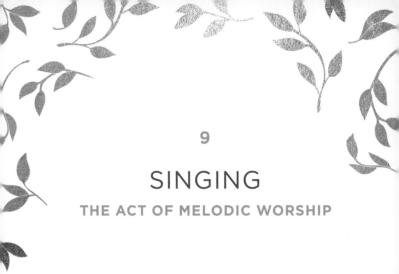

9

SINGING

THE ACT OF MELODIC WORSHIP

Words of adoration combined with a melody from the heart lead to praise in its most beautiful form. Here we discover one of the most neglected aspects of personal worship—singing alone in God's presence. The psalmist enjoined, "Serve the LORD with gladness; come before His presence with singing" (Psalm 100:2).

While many believers freely participate in congregational singing, few have discovered the joy of singing songs unto the Lord *during prayer.* No fewer than forty-one of the psalms specifically refer to "singing praises" unto the Lord. In several of these psalms, you can find three or four separate injunctions to sing. Surely there must be power in giving a personal song offering to the Lord in private prayer.

What should we sing during prayer? On two different occasions Paul spoke of "making melody" in our hearts unto the Lord with "spiritual songs" (Ephesians 5:19; Colossians 3:16). When Paul spoke of a spiritual song he was speaking of a song that originated in the believer's heart. The word *spiritual,* as used in these verses, means "inspired by the Spirit." Paul could not have been referring to the use of hymnbooks in public or private worship since hymnbooks were centuries away from publication when he wrote these words. Undoubtedly, hand-copied psalters were extremely scarce.

We recall also that Paul and Silas "sang praises" unto God while they were in prison (Acts 16:25 KJV). Surely there were no hymnbooks present in this damp cell. Their songs of praise were most certainly based on melodies created in their hearts. To these melodies were added personal words of praise.

The Weapon of Song

Singing unto the Lord during prayer is more than merely a fresh and exciting way to minister unto the Lord. It is actually a weapon of warfare that adds immense power to our praying. Note an Old Testament passage that supports this claim:

In 2 Chronicles 20 we read that Moab, Ammon and the inhabitants of Mount Seir conspired to wage war on King Jehoshaphat of Judah. Upon hearing of the conspiracy, Jehoshaphat called the people of Judah to repentance. From across the nation they gathered for a time of prayer and fasting.

Through Jahaziel the prophet, God promised Jehoshaphat that Judah would see victory in battle. Full details of the battle are described in verses 20–22:

So they rose early in the morning and went out into the Wilderness of Tekoa; and as they went out, Jehoshaphat stood and said, "Hear me, O Judah and you inhabitants of Jerusalem: Believe in the LORD your God, and you shall be established; believe His prophets, and you shall prosper." And when he had consulted with the people, he appointed those who should sing to the LORD, and who should praise the beauty of holiness, as they went out before the army and were saying: "Praise the LORD, For His mercy endures forever." Now *when they began to sing and to praise*, the LORD set ambushes against the

people of Ammon, Moab, and Mount Seir, who had come
against Judah; and they were defeated.

2 Chronicles 20:20–22, emphasis added

Later, the narrative relates that Judah's troops arrived
at the front lines of battle only to discover the enemy was
already defeated. God may have sent angelic hosts to
fight the battle since there is no evidence of other troops
helping Judah win the campaign.

Key to this account are the words of verse 22, "Now
when they began to sing and to praise, the Lord set ambushes. . . ." The victory *began and ended* with musi-
cal worship. So great was the blessing of victory that
Scripture declares, "When Jehoshaphat and his people
came to take away their spoil, they found among them
an abundance of valuables . . . and precious jewelry . . .
more than they could carry away" (2 Chronicles 20:25,
emphasis added).

When the campaign was fully concluded, Jehoshaphat
and the people of Judah named the valley *Berachah*,
which means "blessing." Indeed, the ministry of song
when properly used in the devotional habit is a weapon
that always leads to blessing.

Themes for Song

How do we make singing unto the Lord practical in the daily devotional habit? Of course, the singing of well-known hymns or popular choruses, from memory or with the aid of a hymnbook or chorus sheet, is a possibility. This may, however, tend to add unwanted form to this aspect of prayer, in the same sense that reading someone else's prayers often drains life from our praying.

Rather, ask the Holy Spirit to create new melodies within your heart. With these melodies you will be able to sing songs based on a variety of themes.

The Bible lists at least six distinct themes that might be used in ministering unto the Lord with song. You need not sing songs based on all of these themes during every prayer time, although the list does reveal the vast scriptural foundation for such worship.

Songs of Praise

First, *sing praises unto the Lord*. Such was the worship of Paul and Silas in jail (see Acts 16). The psalmist declared, "Praise the LORD, for the LORD is good; *sing praises to His name*, for it is pleasant" (Psalm 135:3, emphasis added). During this singing phase of prayer, you may wish

Singing unto the Lord
during prayer
is a weapon of warfare
that adds immense power
to our praying.

to sing praises to God instead of speaking them. As suggested, allow the melody to flow from your heart. Do not be concerned if your voice seems somewhat unpleasant.

On a number of occasions when my daughters were younger, they would sing songs to their father. Often these songs were actually composed while they were being sung. Equally often, the presentation was slightly off-key. Yet, I was always delighted when they came to me with their special songs. Each song was special because of the sincerity of heart behind it, and because the singers were objects of their father's affection.

So it is with our spiritual singing. To sing praises unto the Lord brings great joy to God's heart because of His intense love for us.

Songs of Power and Mercy

Second, *sing of God's power and mercy*. "But I will sing of Your power," declared the psalmist. "Yes, I will sing aloud of Your mercy in the morning; for You have been my defense and refuge in the day of my trouble" (Psalm 59:16). Note the psalmist not only speaks of singing, but of singing *aloud*. The thought is that our song is not to be confined only to the heart. It is to be a vocal praising of God with melody.

To sing of God's power is to put into song all that God has accomplished with His power. To sing of His mercy is to sing of His faithfulness and justice. It is to sing the attributes of His divine nature. Indeed, all that God is can become a theme for a personal spiritual song.

Songs of Thanksgiving

Third, *sing a song of thanksgiving*. Look again at the words of the psalmist: "Sing to the LORD *with thanksgiving*; sing praises on the harp to our God" (Psalm 147:7, emphasis added). As suggested in earlier chapters, praise is to recognize God for who He is. Thanksgiving, on the other hand, is to recognize God for what He has done for us. In singing "with thanksgiving" we create a song based on those specific gifts or blessings God has provided.

Sadly, few believers have ever experienced the joy of thanking God in song for little things like food and clothing. Anything we can thank God for verbally, we can thank God for musically.

Songs of God's Name

Fourth, *sing the name of God*. To sing the name of the Lord in a song is scriptural. The psalmist testified, "I will praise the name of God with a song, and will magnify Him with thanksgiving" (Psalm 69:30).

As suggested in our earlier discussion of praise, the "name" of the Lord in the Old Testament may be a direct reference to the name God took upon Himself when coming to earth in the form of His Son. The Bible says, "God was in Christ" when He reconciled the world (2 Corinthians 5:19).

This makes it possible to praise the name of the Lord Jesus Christ in song. All that Jesus is or did can become the theme of our singing during our time alone in God's presence.

Songs of God's Word

Fifth, *sing God's Word*. The psalmist speaks once again of the power of song: "Your statutes have been my songs in the house of my pilgrimage" (Psalm 119:54). To put melody to God's Word is another excellent way to worship God in song. We know that Christians of the early Church were admonished to sing Scripture. James advised, "Is anyone among you suffering? Let him pray. Is anyone cheerful? Let him sing psalms" (James 5:13). Surely this admonition does not apply only to singing in a gathering of believers. A person can be afflicted alone as well as with the congregation. If alone and afflicted, a person is to pray. Similarly, if *any* (note the emphasis on the singular) *is merry, let him or her sing.* Any believer who is happy in Christ has at least one theme for a personal song during prayer. One's joy can be expressed in a spiritual song.

Songs of My Heart

Finally, *sing a new song.* The psalmist shared, "I will sing a new song to You, O God; on a harp of ten strings I will sing praises to You" (Psalm 144:9). "New" refers to something fresh. "A new song" means "my own song," not someone else's. It refers to a song from my heart that I have never sung before. Yesterday's song does not qualify under this category of singing. The theme may be similar but the song will be new. Of course, all the various themes for singing may fall under this category if we have never sung the melody or words previously. Even the singing of a Scripture in a new way can be a "new song" from my heart.

To sing praises unto the Lord
brings great joy to God's heart
because of His intense love for us.

Only the imagination can limit our singing "new songs" unto the Lord. Singing unto the Lord is especially important because it trains us in many new areas of worship. Ultimately, worship will be our *eternal purpose in heaven*, and singing will be a great part of this eternal purpose. In fact, note the description Isaiah gives of believers entering Zion, "Therefore the redeemed of the LORD shall return, and come with singing unto Zion; and everlasting joy shall be upon their head: they shall obtain gladness and joy; and sorrow and mourning shall flee away" (Isaiah 51:11 KJV).

If singing is to play so vital a role in heaven's worship, surely it would do the believer well to "practice up" for the day we unite together in heavenly song to minister unto the Lord in our eternal Zion.

Lord, teach me to sing!

Singing: The Ninth Step in World-Changing Prayer

1. Pause to sing a spontaneous song to the Lord.

2. Select a special theme for your song, such as praise, thanksgiving or a favorite passage of

Scripture. Don't hesitate to include thanks for specific blessings or victories you believe God will give you in the days ahead.

3. Then, ask the Holy Spirit to create an original melody in your heart so your song is "a new song." Use a melody of a familiar song if needed.

4. Put the new words and melody together and sing!

PRAYER

Creator, Father, Lord of all, I lift my voice to sing praise to Your name and bring You glory and honor. Let my song rise to You as an original sacrifice of praise, an offering of thanksgiving, a sweet sound to Your ears. You are my Refuge, my Help, my Safe Place, my Deliverer. I sing to You for all You have been, all You are, all You will forever be.

SCRIPTURES TO SING

Deuteronomy 32:3–4; Psalm 18:1–3, 30–36; Psalm 95:1–7; Revelation 7:12

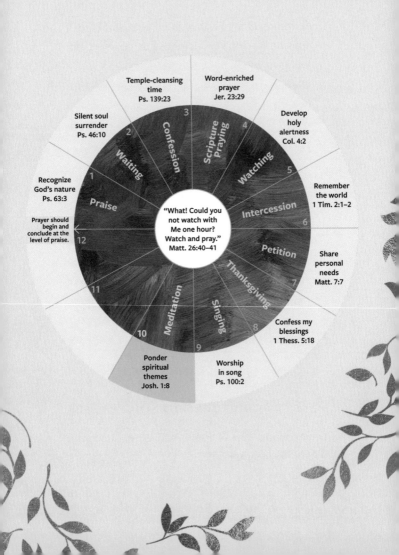

Temple-cleansing
time
Ps. 139:23

Word-enriched
prayer
Jer. 23:29

Silent soul
surrender
Ps. 46:10

Develop
holy
alertness
Col. 4:2

Recognize
God's nature
Ps. 63:3

Remember
the world
1 Tim. 2:1–2

Prayer should
begin and
conclude at the
level of praise.

Share
personal
needs
Matt. 7:7

Confess my
blessings
1 Thess. 5:18

Ponder
spiritual
themes
Josh. 1:8

Worship
in song
Ps. 100:2

3 Confession

4 Scripture Praying

2 Waiting

Watching

5

1 Praise

Intercession

6

12

Petition

"What! Could you
not watch with
Me one hour?
Watch and pray."
Matt. 26:40–41

11

Thanksgiving

7

Meditation

Singing

10

9

8

10

MEDITATION

THE ACT OF SPIRITUAL EVALUATION

The devotional hour is greatly strengthened when the believer takes time to ponder a spiritual theme in reference to God. This act of spiritual evaluation, called meditation, helps the believer discover how to apply all the truths God has revealed during prayer.

The Old Testament definition for the word *meditation* is "to mutter" or "to muse." This suggests a silent inner study of some spiritual matter. This is the essence of the meaning of "meditate" in Joshua 1:8: "This Book of the Law shall not depart from your mouth, but you shall meditate in it day and night, that you may observe to do according to all that is written in it. For then you will make your way prosperous, and then you will have good success." Here, the Hebrew word for "meditate" (*hagah*) means "to mutter upon."

Another Hebrew expression translated "meditate" is *sicah*, which means "to bow down." The psalmist used this word when declaring, "I will meditate on Your precepts, and contemplate Your ways" (Psalm 119:15). The thought is that we render special "mental attention" by bowing down in respect of God's Word.

In the New Testament, meditation is emphasized in Paul's admonition to Timothy, "Meditate on these things; give yourself entirely to them, that your progress may be evident to all" (1 Timothy 4:15). In this verse the Greek word for "meditate," *meletao*, means "to be careful," or "to show care" in a matter. This suggests meditation is more than merely thinking good thoughts. It is the giving of attention to how we might specifically apply these ponderings after the devotional hour has ended.

The Value of Meditation

Scriptural meditation provides the believer with spiritual benefits received through no other means. Personal inner peace is but one of these benefits. The Bible promises,

"You will keep him in perfect peace, whose mind is stayed on You" (Isaiah 26:3).

Throughout Scripture frequent attention is given to this matter of meditation: "How precious also are Your thoughts to me, O God! How great is the sum of them! If I should count them, they would be more in number than the sand; when I awake, I am still with You" (Psalm 139:17–18).

Earlier the psalmist declared, "May my meditation be sweet to Him; I will be glad in the LORD" (Psalm 104:34). He also declared, "In the multitude of my anxieties within me, Your comforts delight my soul" (Psalm 94:19).

The person who spends time thinking thoughts of God will find tremendous depth and understanding that will touch all areas of his or her life. It is, after all, in meditation that we rise above ourselves (and the world) for the purpose of seeing God's plan in proper perspective. Only from such a vantage point can we see the spiritual realm clearly.

Meditation is equally meaningful because it allows the believer to cultivate a harvest of fresh creative thoughts. As Oliver Wendell Holmes explained, "Every now and then a man's mind is stretched by a new idea . . . and never shrinks back to its former dimensions."[1]

Meditating with a solidly biblical foundation is the best thinking in which humans can engage. Scripture provides the believer with a meaningful list of practical themes upon which to focus our meditation. Like other suggestions shared in these chapters, it is not necessary to implement all of these types of meditation during every devotional hour. However, the list is practical because it is scriptural. For a well-balanced devotional hour, select at least one aspect each day as a focus for your meditation.

Focus on God Himself

First, *focus meditation on God Himself*. Speaking of meditation the psalmist declared, "My soul, wait silently for God alone, for my expectation is from Him" (Psalm 62:5).

Earlier it was suggested that the believer take time to wait in prayer for the purpose of focusing love entirely upon God. Now we return in prayer to enlarge that focus. At first glance it may appear that waiting and meditation overlap in their functions. However, *waiting* is an act of loving, while *meditation* is an act of thinking.

During this particular type of meditation, ponder the nature of God with full intensity. Carefully probe everything you know about your heavenly Father, constantly asking the Holy Spirit to illuminate and stretch your thinking.

In the course of this type of meditation you will often find yourself asking many questions. What do I really believe about God? What does the Bible say about God that touches my life? How would I define my concept of God? What great attributes of God can I better appropriate in my daily life? As you answer these and other questions about God, your understanding of His nature and purpose increases dramatically, as does your confidence in His Word.

Focus on God's Word

Second, *focus meditation on God's Word*. The first two verses of the Psalms lead us to this focus of meditation: "Blessed is the man who walks not in the counsel of the ungodly, nor stands in the path of sinners, nor sits in the seat of the scornful; but his delight is in the law of the LORD, and in His law he meditates day and night" (Psalm 1:1–2).

Because meditation is the mental evaluation of any spiritual theme, the Bible becomes a tremendous source for meditation. Scripture is filled with thousands of brief phrases that inspire enormous power. Altogether, nearly thirty thousand promises await us in Scripture. Each promise can be a focus for meditation.

Focus on God's Works

Third, *focus meditation on the works of God*. The psalmist expressed, "I will also meditate on all Your work, and talk of Your deeds" (Psalm 77:12). Here is another form of meditation that proves limitless. Every created aspect of the universe can become a focal point for effective meditation. But always, these ponderings must be in reference to God. We do not meditate on the beauty of a mountain stream simply because of the stream's beauty, but because of the stream's Creator.

Focus on Past Victories

Fourth, *focus meditation on past victories*. Here is a seldom-mentioned aspect of meditation that will provide an oasis of delight for your devotional hour. The psalmist shared succinctly, "I remember the days of old" (Psalm 143:5). In times of distress and discouragement, much spiritual relief can be found in looking at the many blessings God has given us in previous days.

Consider Jeremiah's difficult experiences as recorded in Lamentations. Indeed, the very word *lamentation* means brokenness, pain, or grief. Of the five painful chapters in the book, perhaps the most distressing is chapter 3. Here the prophet speaks of God pulling him in pieces and of all his bones being broken. A particularly graphic verse reads, "He has also broken my teeth with gravel, and covered me with ashes" (Lamentations 3:16).

But notice the pause in the narrative that transforms Jeremiah's desert experience into a garden of blessings. In the midst of his complaints the prophet declares, "*This I recall to my mind*, therefore I have hope. Through the LORD's mercies we are not consumed, because His compassions fail not. They are new every morning; great is Your faithfulness" (Lamentations 3:21–23, emphasis added).

Jeremiah discovered the secret of retrospective meditation. "This I recall," the prophet wrote during his battle with depression. When he had reached the point of total defeat he reflected on the past faithfulness of God. Because of this, Jeremiah was able to testify, "Great is Your faithfulness!"

We can do little during prayer that will add more beauty and freshness to our daily experience than will a moment set aside to ponder past victories in Jesus. Sometimes a former experience will come alive with such reality that we almost relive the experience. The end result is a new confidence to face even the most difficult future.

Focus on Positive Thoughts

Finally, *focus meditation on positive thoughts*. Paul told his Philippian friends, "Finally, brethren, whatever things are true, whatever things are noble, whatever things are just, whatever things are pure, whatever things are lovely, whatever things are of good report, if there is any virtue and if there is anything praiseworthy—meditate on these things" (Philippians 4:8).

Anything worthy of praise is worthy of meditation. For example, some people especially love little children. They may see the glory of God in a baby's eyes. Let them begin their time of meditation by setting a small child— perhaps the child they love best—in the midst of their many thoughts.

Any thought that meets the measure of Philippians 4:8 may serve as a focus for meditation. Teaching received in a Sunday school class or excerpts from a Christian podcast make excellent food for meditation. Even a distraction during prayer may serve as fuel to ignite the flames of meaningful meditation.

If, during your time of spiritual evaluation, a distressing thought repeatedly buffets the mind, make that thought a special point for meditation. With God's help, walk through the problem step by step until a solution is discovered. Soon, meditation will become a practical way to visualize new avenues for sound spiritual growth.

Lord, teach me to meditate!

Meditation: The Tenth Step in World-Changing Prayer

1. Select a theme for your time of meditation, applying full attention to that specific area of spiritual thought.

2. Allow your mind to wander within the framework of your chosen theme. Ponder all aspects of the theme in reference to God.

3. Ask yourself questions about this theme that might lead you into an even deeper mental study of the subject.

4. Bring Scripture into all phases of meditation. This strengthens your awareness that God's Word is the necessary foundation for all meaningful spiritual thought.

 **PRAYER**

Today, God, I am focusing on how You provide our planet and all humanity with water. You made a way for our thirst to be nourished, for plants to grow and food to replenish, and for bodies of water to refill through evaporation and rain. I am reminded of Psalm 104:10–11, where David wrote that You send "springs into the valleys . . . they give drink to every beast of the field," and Job 5:10 that says You send rain and water to the earth. Jesus, You invite us to come to You and drink when we are thirsty. Let Your rivers of living water flow from my heart (John 7:37–39). As I ponder how You have provided

for the planet as a whole, I know that You will also provide for me.

SCRIPTURES TO PRAY

Joshua 1:8; Psalm 63:6; Psalm 119:15; Matthew 6:25–34; Colossians 3:1–2

Temple-cleansing
time
Ps. 139:23

Word-enriched
prayer
Jer. 23:29

Silent soul
surrender
Ps. 46:10

Develop
holy
alertness
Col. 4:2

Recognize
God's nature
Ps. 63:3

Remember
the world
1 Tim. 2:1–2

Prayer should
begin and
conclude at the
level of praise.

"What! Could you
not watch with
Me one hour?
Watch and pray."
Matt. 26:40–41

Share
personal
needs
Matt. 7:7

Receive
spiritual
instruction
Eccl. 5:2

Confess my
blessings
1 Thess. 5:18

Ponder
spiritual
themes
Josh. 1:8

Worship
in song
Ps. 100:2

1 Praise
2 Waiting
3 Confession
4 Scripture Praying
5 Watching
6 Intercession
7 Petition
8 Thanksgiving
9 Singing
10 Meditation
11 Listening
12

11

LISTENING

THE ACT OF MENTAL ABSORPTION

"Prayer is the soul's pilgrimage from self to God; and the most effectual remedy for self-love and self-absorption is the habit of humble listening."[1] These words, written over a century ago, bring us to that element of prayer called *listening*. Many centuries earlier, Solomon penned, "Do not be rash with your mouth, and let not your heart utter anything hastily before God. For God is in heaven, and you on earth; therefore let your words be few" (Ecclesiastes 5:2).

In our study of the devotional hour, it becomes evident that certain elements of prayer seem quite similar. Some might wonder how listening differs from either waiting or meditation.

As stated, waiting is to thoughtfully focus attention on God in a love relationship. It is a time of resting silently in God's love. On the other hand, meditation is a very careful exploration of a particular spiritual theme. Though closely related to both, listening is an element of prayer that stands alone. To listen in prayer is to mentally absorb divine instructions from God concerning specific matters for that day.

Best friends are always good listeners. If we truly desire to be friends with the Lord, we must learn the secret of listening. Not only did Jesus say He would enter the open door of a person's heart, but He promised to "sup" with that person as well (Revelation 3:20 KJV). To sup means to have fellowship. Much of our praying consists of *asking* instead of supping. Prayer often becomes one-sided and self-centered. Our prayer should be a conversation, one in which we listen as much as we speak.

In a certain sense, listening is an actual ministry. Jesus ministered through listening. As Hope MacDonald explains in *Discovering How to Pray*, "Jesus listened to the cry of the blind man in the crowded noisy street. He listened to the story of Mary Magdalene when she came uninvited to a dinner party. He listened to the plea of the lepers when no one else would go near them. Jesus also listened to Nicodemus, who came to talk to Him late one night. Our Lord even listened to the thief hanging next to Him when He was dying on the cross."[2]

To be like Jesus is to be a listener, especially in prayer. The desire of Jesus was to do the will of His Father. To find His Father's will, Jesus spent whole nights listening. We, too, must follow the example of Jesus and learn the art of listening.

The Gift of Listening

To quiet our hearts for the specific purpose of receiving the day's guidance is an act of both dependence and faith. Listening implies confidence that God truly desires to speak to us. It also serves to move our devotional habit still further from an emphasis on self. As we learn to hear the voice of the Father, we also learn to dispel the voices of the world.

Of necessity, much of prayer must take place in silence because much of prayer concerns the believer seeking divine guidance. Not only will God reveal how to pray

Best friends
are always good listeners.
If we truly desire to be
friends with the Lord,
we must learn the secret
of listening.

effectively, if we will listen, but He will reveal how to *live* effectively.

God alone knows the solution to every problem we will face. This listening phase of prayer allows the believer to tune in on God's solutions. Carefully guard your devotional hour from becoming a soliloquy of selfishness. We do not engage in prayer to tell God what to do. Our goal in prayer is to discover what God wants us to do so that He will be glorified.

The Price of Silence

God mightily used Moses because he was "very humble." More than this, as Scripture relates, Moses was humble "more than all men who were on the face of the earth" (Numbers 12:3). Here was an old man, eighty years of age, and yet God chose Moses to lead an army of several million. Why? Because Moses was "humble," and the humble person is a listener.

Awesome power awaits the Christian who develops a listener's spirit. But because this spirit leads to such power, the price to obtain it is high. Describing this spirit, Peter relates, "A gentle and quiet spirit . . . is very precious in the sight of God" (1 Peter 3:4).

What is the price of silence, but the gift of self to God? It is to shut our eyes to what the world considers important and listen only to the Holy Spirit's call. The price of silence is also time, much time given to the practice of listening.

In an active world nothing seems more difficult than "soul listening." The closer we come to the conclusion of our devotional hour, the more our minds cry out for action. Let us listen carefully to be certain all of our plans for action originate in God.

Since the sounds of the world wreak havoc in our prayer, the secret of silence begins in conquering these undesirable sounds.

How will God speak during these times of stillness? Often His whisperings come in the form of a quiet impression on the heart. Elijah heard God speak with the "sound of a gentle whisper" (1 Kings 19:12 NLT). But His whispering was very specific, as God gave Elijah guidance for that particular moment in his experience.

On other occasions there is no inner voice to guide us, yet we sense God's presence gently leading. We know that to move in a certain direction will please God, and so we follow this quiet leading.

Most often God speaks through His Word. In fact, all forms of guidance must be measured by Scripture.

Guidance contrary to God's Word is guidance originating from another source.

During the listening aspect of prayer you may wish to keep a notepad handy to record these impressions concerning your day. If a stay-at-home mother asks God to help her plan the day's activities, she should be ready to jot down any divine promptings. The businessperson who questions which important project demands the most careful attention for the day should ask God to give specific wisdom for that day's responsibilities.

Always remember, listening serves a practical function. You are not merely listening for divine "niceties," but you are asking God to order your day. The value of having paper and pencil or a notepad app is that it displays faith. It says to God, "I believe You will truly speak to me, and I have come prepared to record Your instructions."

True, there are dangers to be faced when we enter these deeper aspects of prayer. Much of prayer is an experiment in spiritual growth that involves both failure and success. But if we persevere, the blessings will transcend all disappointments. Our knowledge of God will increase and abound beyond measure.

Lord, teach me to listen!

Listening: The Eleventh Step in World-Changing Prayer

1. Before you listen in prayer, ask God what He wants to say to you today. Then ask very specific questions about difficult problems or situations that need a solution.

2. Search Scripture for specific answers to your questions. One way God will speak to you is through His Word.

3. Mentally evaluate all circumstances that relate to a problem. Ask God to show you His plan through those circumstances.

4. Write down any ideas God may share concerning the details of solving that particular problem.

 PRAYER

Thank You for being ever-present and wanting to speak to me. I am struggling with ___ today, and I am not sure how to handle it. Psalm 46:1–3 says You are my "refuge and strength" and that You will always be with me in times of trouble. In 1 Corinthians

2:10, I read that You reveal the mysteries of Your wisdom through the Holy Spirit. I need that wisdom today and humbly ask You to reveal it to me. I wait for Your voice and Your guidance as I think through Your will for me.

SCRIPTURES TO PRAY

Deuteronomy 32:1–2; Psalm 25:4; Psalm 37:7; Jeremiah 33:3

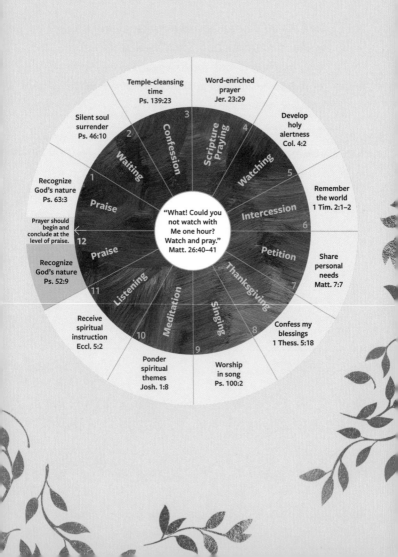

Temple-cleansing time
Ps. 139:23

Word-enriched prayer
Jer. 23:29

Silent soul surrender
Ps. 46:10

Develop holy alertness
Col. 4:2

Recognize God's nature
Ps. 63:3

Remember the world
1 Tim. 2:1–2

Prayer should begin and conclude at the level of praise.

Share personal needs
Matt. 7:7

Recognize God's nature
Ps. 52:9

Confess my blessings
1 Thess. 5:18

Receive spiritual instruction
Eccl. 5:2

Worship in song
Ps. 100:2

Ponder spiritual themes
Josh. 1:8

3 Confession

Scripture Praying 4

Waiting 2

Watching 5

Praise 1

Intercession

Praise 12

Petition 6

Listening 11

Thanksgiving

Meditation

Singing 7

10

9

8

"What! Could you not watch with Me one hour? Watch and pray."
Matt. 26:40–41

PRAISE

THE ACT OF DIVINE MAGNIFICATION

Prayer has now come full circle, and we find ourselves again at praise. Worship should seal all praying. We began with an act of adoration, and we will end with an act of magnification.

When Mary received word she would give birth to the Son of God, divine worship exploded from her lips: "My soul magnifies the Lord, and my spirit has rejoiced in God my Savior. For He who is mighty has done great things for me, and holy is His name" (Luke 1:46–47, 49).

Jesus not only taught us to begin our prayer with praise—"Our Father in heaven, hallowed be Your name"— but He also taught us to end our praying with praise— "For

Yours is the kingdom and the power and the glory forever. Amen" (Matthew 6:9, 13).

Prayer's Final Moments

As we come to these final moments of prayer, the soul pauses to contemplate the awesome wonder of God's being. We vocally magnify the nature of God. To magnify the Lord's name with praise is to put a spiritual magnifying glass to all that God is and declare these discoveries aloud.

The Greek word for magnify in Luke 1:46, *megaluno*, means "to make great." Nothing could provide so meaningful a conclusion to prayer as a statement of the greatness of God. With the psalmist we declare, "Great is the LORD, and greatly to be praised" (Psalm 48:1).

As prayer concludes, we praise God because it has been His greatness that has made our devotional hour possible. When we began praying, we recognized God's glory in all of its splendor and beauty. Now we restate our case for worship. In these final moments, we add faith to our praise. We actually praise God for future answers to prayer. With the psalmist we declare, "I will praise You forever, *because You have done it*" (Psalm 52:9, emphasis added).

Because every day must be lived in a spirit of praise, the specific practice of praise just before concluding prayer is essential. It prepares us for our highest function in life—to minister unto the Lord continuously.

Praise in the closet also prepares us to conquer our foes outside the closet. Paul Billheimer concludes, "Praise is the most useful occupation and activity in enabling God to realize the supreme goal of the Universe, that of 'bringing many sons into glory.'"[1]

The bringing of lost souls to glory is the ultimate focal point for all prayer and praise. We *pray*, "Your Kingdom come," and we *praise*, "For Yours is the kingdom." Although much can be said about prayer, bringing glory to God is at the center of it. When Jesus told His disciples, "You will ask what you desire, and it shall be done for you," He added, "By this My Father is glorified" (John 15:7–8). God must be glorified through our praying, and praise enables the prayer warrior to keep this thought continually in focus.

The Attitude of Prayer

Perhaps the greatest secret to learn about prayer is how to maintain a devotional attitude after the devotional hour concludes. We must learn to take the spirit of praise with us from the prayer closet. No amount of prayer holds value if the prayer warrior remains unchanged.

Seize God's power during these closing moments of worship. Let an attitude of prayer flood your being as you prepare for your day. Always remember, God has been your power during prayer and will be your power throughout the day.

Jesus taught us to conclude our praying with the expression, "Amen" (Matthew 6:13). It means "so be it" or "it is done." A student of Greek told me that *amen* could actually be translated "God, our King, is trustworthy." To say "amen" in prayer is to express confidence that God has heard our petitions.

Martin Luther was known for his bold, almost brash petitioning of God. Yet Luther saw many dramatic answers to prayer. A friend once said of the reformation leader, "What a spirit, what a confidence was in his very expressions. With such a reverence he sued as one begging God, and yet with such hope and assurance, as if he spoke with a loving father or friend."[2]

It was Martin Luther who said of prayer's conclusion, "Mark this! Make your amen *strong*, never doubting that God is surely listening to you. This is what amen means:

No amount of prayer
holds value
if the prayer warrior
remains unchanged.
Take the spirit of praise
with you from the prayer closet.

That I know with certainty that this prayer has been heard by God."[3]

We, too, should end our praying with a strong expression of confidence. Paraphrase your "amen" with a testimony of faith. Say, "God, I know You can be trusted to bring these petitions into being. I confess my confidence in Your promises. I praise You because it is done!"

The Gift of Praise

Thus, our devoted prayer time with God has ended. We have not finished our praying with a list of personal petitions but with a spirit of grateful praise. When we leave the closet, we are not asking, but giving. Prayer has concluded with an offering of our lips. With the psalmist we have declared, "Accept, I pray, the freewill offerings of my mouth" (Psalm 119:108).

Into a busy world we carry these words of divine magnification. Our goal beyond the closet is to magnify God's name in all we do. Every action will be sprinkled with silent worship. His praise shall be the very object of our conversation. The greatness of God shall dominate all thought and conduct.

Lord, teach me to magnify You!

Praise: The Twelfth Step in World-Changing Prayer

1. End your prayer with specific praise concerning God's greatness. Focus your praise on His omnipotence (power), His omniscience (knowledge) and His omnipresence (presence).

2. With the psalmist let us "praise God because He has done it." Look back at your time of prayer and praise God for hearing each of your requests.

3. Let your spirit rejoice for a few moments at the close of prayer. Repeat the universal word for praise, *Hallelujah!*

4. As Martin Luther suggested, when your time of prayer concludes, make your "amen" strong. Confess with authority that you believe God is trustworthy.

 **PRAYER**

O Lord, my God, I am in awe of who You are. You are the powerful Creator, full of wisdom and always near. None compares to You. I praise You for

allowing me to bring each of my requests to You today, and for Your answers to each. Your greatness, Your love toward me and Your willingness to spend time with me overwhelm me with gratefulness. I praise You with all my being. Hallelujah to the Lord of lords! Hallelujah! I believe that You will do all You have promised and I trust in You, my King, Amen!

SCRIPTURES TO PRAY

1 Chronicles 16:29; Psalm 99:5; Psalm 117:1–2; Hebrews 13:15

Scriptural Intercession and Practical Involvement

YOUR INVITATION TO BE A "WATCHMAN WARRIOR"

We know it is a good thing to pray for others, especially the millions living in unevangelized nations. But how can we be assured that our praying is truly scriptural?

Scriptural prayer for world evangelism basically centers in four areas. We might label these areas the "four claims" for world-changing prayer.

First, *claim workers for the harvest*. Find prayer resources available at EHC.org or OperationWorld.org. Prior to "making mention" of the various nations in prayer, vocally claim each of these four scriptural items. I include the claim for workers first because Jesus included it first. Of all Christ taught in the gospels, only once do we find Him sharing the ultimate solution to all problems of world evangelism.

Having painted the picture of a vast harvest, Jesus shares His only plan for reaping the harvest: "Therefore beseech the Lord of the harvest to send out workers into His harvest" (Matthew 9:38 NASB).

Nothing is more important in the worldwide work of God than those workers who shoulder the responsibilities of the harvest. God's plan centers in people. People who know Jesus must share this knowledge with people who do not know Jesus. It is true that only God can give the "increase" (1 Corinthians 3:6), but it is equally true that God will allow no increase without humanity's involvement. Augustine expressed it well: "Without God, we cannot, but without us, God will not!"[1]

Second, *claim open doors*. It is also scriptural to claim open doors for those workers who serve in the Lord's harvest. Indeed, the workers we claimed a moment ago will accomplish nothing if they have no field of labor. Even ten thousand qualified workers would accomplish very little in a nation where laws totally prohibit evangelistic activity. One-third of the earth's population live under just such restrictions. This is why Paul told the Colossians, "Devote yourselves to prayer . . . that God will open up . . . a door for the word" (Colossians 4:2–3 NASB).

To "devote" suggests we give ourselves earnestly to intercession for open doors of ministry. We should pray especially for specific leaders of nations who hold in their political hands the power to permit evangelistic outreach and church worship.

Paul told Timothy, "Therefore I exhort first of all that supplications, prayers, intercessions, and giving of thanks be made for all men, for kings and all who are in authority" (1 Timothy 2:1–2).

Paul knew that evangelizing every nation is possible only if these leaders permit the peaceful spread of the gospel. Thus, he instructed us to pray for all those in authority.

Third, *claim "fruit" that will remain*. Paul greatly desired that his efforts would not be in vain. "I desire fruit," he declared (Philippians 4:17 KJV). Of the Thessalonians Paul also requested, "Finally, brethren, pray for us, that the word of the Lord may run swiftly *and be glorified*" (2 Thessalonians 3:1, emphasis added). Paul longed that nothing would hinder the swift accomplishment of those goals God had given him. But more than that, he desired that every spiritual seed planted would take deep root.

Take time during prayer to lift those of Christ's body involved in caring for new converts. In many cultures a convert is rejected by both family and society. Without help the young believer finds it almost impossible to survive spiritually. Our prayers of intercession can actually make the difference.

Fourth, *claim a strong base of support for missionary outreach*. The Bible stresses the importance of sending forth workers. Of course, the sending forth of these workers bears a price tag. After declaring that all who call upon the name of the Lord shall be saved, Paul stressed the need for workers to convey this message. Paul asked the Roman believers, "How then shall they call on Him in whom they have not believed? And how shall they believe in Him of whom they have not heard? And how shall they hear without a preacher? And how shall they preach *unless they are sent?*" (Romans 10:14–15, emphasis added).

The sending forth of workers properly equipped with all the necessary tools can be a very costly matter. Psalm 2:8 speaks of the lost being reached in the "ends of the earth." Having spent many hours meditating on the difficult aspects of world evangelism and traveling to remote places like Communist China, I am convinced that many

Christians do not comprehend the enormous monetary responsibility in reaching these "ends of the earth."

For example, consider the thousands of islands that dot the world's oceans. Each must be visited by messengers of God's love. None can be overlooked. Jesus commissioned us to go into "all the world" (Mark 16:15).

But how costly and involved will this task be? Indonesia provides an excellent example. The fourth most populated country in the world, with 272 million people, Indonesia has a remarkable 17,000 separate islands (of which 3,000 are inhabited). Consider further that many islands include only a handful of inhabitants. In visiting both the Indonesian and Philippine island chains, Every Home for Christ workers have traveled entire days by boat to share printed gospel messages with only ten or twelve families *on a single island*. But until all are reached, the completion of the Great Commission is only a spiritual dream. To claim a strong base of support for evangelistic endeavors and to become a part of that base, is to hasten the day of total world evangelization.

The Destiny of Our Neighbors and Nations

Beloved, it is not age, experience, talent or material wealth that makes the difference in the destiny of men and nations. Prayer alone will change the world, from our neighbors to the nations.

It is true that God may use age, experience, talent and material wealth to help carry forth His purposes, but only when each is properly backed by prayer. Without prayer, every effort is wasted, for it leaves God out of the picture. Wise is the statement that there is much we can do *after* we have prayed but nothing we can do *until* we have prayed. Thus, all of our questions are reduced to one: Will I say yes to the supreme plea of Jesus to watch with Him one hour? To say yes today, and every day, not only releases power into a neglected world, but it aligns me with the very ministry Jesus carries on *today*. Scripture says, "He always lives to make intercession" (Hebrews 7:25).

Nothing I can do will please Christ more than my joining with Him in daily prayer. And when I do, something happens in the world, including my neighborhood, school or workplace, that could not happen through any other means. My hour with Jesus, though brief in comparison to the ages of recorded time, actually makes a difference in the events that constitute these ages.

So, once again let our hearts stand silent as Jesus softly asks, "What, could you not watch with Me one hour?" It is a question each must answer, and on that answer hangs the destiny of my neighbors and the nations.

Lord, teach me to "always pray and not give up"! (Luke 18:1 NLT).

Notes

Chapter 2: Waiting

1. E. M. Bounds, *The Weapon of Prayer* (Grand Rapids: Baker, 1975), 156.
2. Norman Pittenger, *Praying Today* (Grand Rapids: Wm. B. Eerdmans, 1974), 35.
3. Andrew Murray, *The Prayer Life* (Chicago: Moody, n.d.), 43.

Chapter 3: Confession

1. Andrew Murray, *The Prayer Life* (Chicago: Moody, n.d.), 117.
2. D. L. Moody, *Prevailing Prayer* (Chicago: Moody, n.d.), 36–37.

Chapter 4: Scripture Praying

1. E. M. Bounds, *The Necessity of Prayer* (Grand Rapids: Baker, 1976), 10.
2. George Mueller, *An Autobiography of George Mueller* (London: J. Nisbet, 1906), 150.
3. E. M. Bounds, *The Possibilities of Prayer* (Minneapolis: Bethany, 1978).
4. J. Oswald Sanders, *Prayer Power Unlimited* (Chicago: Moody, 1977), 9.

Chapter 5: Watching

1. Dick Eastman, Every Home for Christ, http://www.ehc.org.
2. Ole Hallesby, *Prayer* (Minneapolis: Augsburg, 1931), 36.

Chapter 6: Intercession

1. From a message given by Dr. Lee at a World Literature Crusade global conference, Friday, March 11, 1983, Chatsworth, California.
2. Belle Marvel Brain, *Holding the Ropes: Missionary Methods for Workers at Home* (New York: Funk & Wagnalls, 1904), 211.
3. Some readers may wonder why two common prayer terms—*travail* and *supplication*—are not listed in our discussion as specific elements of the devotional habit. *Travail* is an intense form of intercession, whereas *supplication* is an intense form of petition. Thus, to plead with great intensity for a personal need is a type of petition called *supplication*. To plead with great intensity for the needs of another is a type of intercessory prayer called *travail*. The author's earlier book on prayer, *No Easy Road: Inspirational Thoughts on Prayer* (Grand Rapids: Chosen Books, 2003), presents a look at both supplication and travail in relationship to prayer.
4. Edwin and Lillian Harvey, *Kneeling We Triumph* (Chicago: Moody, 1974), 40.
5. Anne J. Townsend, *Prayer without Pretending* (Chicago: Moody, 1973), 82.
6. The apostle Paul also referred to "making mention" of fellow workers in prayer in Ephesians 1:16, Philippians 1:3–4, and 1 Thessalonians 1:2.

Chapter 7: Petition

1. Charles H. Spurgeon, *Twelve Sermons on Prayer* (Grand Rapids: Baker, 1971), 99.

Chapter 10: Meditation

1. Oliver Wendell Holmes, "The Autocrat of the Breakfast Table," *Atlantic Monthly*, Volume 2 (Boston: Phillips, Sampson and Company, September 1858), 502, https://books.google.com/books?id=BoQ3AQ AAMAAJ.

Chapter 11: Listening

1. Bridgid E. Herman, *Christian Prayer* (New York: Harper and Row, n.d.), 25.

2. Hope MacDonald, *Discovering How to Pray* (Grand Rapids: Zondervan, 1976), 53–54.

Chapter 12: Praise

1. Paul E. Billheimer, *Destined for the Throne* (Fort Washington, Penn.: Christian Literature Crusade, 1957), 117.

2. J. C. Ryle, *A Call to Prayer* (Grand Rapids: Baker, 1976), 68.

3. Martin Luther, *Luther's Works: Devotional Writings*, vol. 43 of *Luther's Works*, ed. Jaroslav Pelikan (St. Louis: Concordia Publishing House, 1955), 198.

Scriptural Intercession and Practical Involvement

1. Norman Pittenger, *Praying Today* (Grand Rapids: Wm. B. Eerdmans, 1974), 152.

Dr. Dick Eastman is the international president of Every Home for Christ, a ministry that has planted over 4.5 billion gospel messages home to home worldwide since 1946, resulting in over 240 million followed-up decision cards and responses and nearly 400,000 church fellowships called Christ Groups.

In his role with Every Home for Christ, Dick has traveled around the world more than 100 times. He also serves as president of America's National Prayer Committee, a diverse group of evangelical leaders instrumental in planning America's annual National Day of Prayer (scheduled by Congressional decree for the first Thursday of May each year). As president of the National Prayer Committee, Dick has been invited to the White House as the guest of former Presidents Ronald Reagan, George Bush, Bill Clinton, and George W. Bush.

Dick is the originator of the Change the World School of Prayer, a multipart seminar that has trained more than 2,000,000 Christians in 120 nations on the power and intimacy of prayer. He is also the author of numerous bestselling books on prayer and evangelism, including *The Hour That Changes the World* and *Look What God Is Doing!*, which have sold more than two million copies.

Dick Eastman and his wife, Dee, make their home in Colorado Springs, Colorado, and have two grown daughters and nine grandchildren.

Free resources to grow your prayer life...

1. Pray for every nation on earth each month using Every Home for Christ's **World Prayer Map**.
2. Pray for a national revival and awakening in the USA using EHC's **United States Prayer Map**.
3. Read about signs and wonders and other accounts of God's miraculous work in history's greatest harvests in *Look What God Is Doing!*